The Complete Book of Sandwiches
for the Professional Chef®

Terence Janericco

CBI Publishing Company, Inc.
286 Congress Street
Boston, Massachusetts 02210

Production Editor / Rebecca Handler
Text Designer / Designed For
Compositor / Arabesque Composition
Cover Designer / Christy Rosso
Cover and Interior Photographs /
Terence Janericco

Library of Congress Cataloging in Publication Data

Janericco, Terence.
   The complete book of sandwiches for the profes-
sional chef.

   Includes index.
   1. Sandwiches.   2. Quantity cookery.   I. Title.
TX818.J35   1983   641.8′4   83-6421
ISBN 0-8436-2270-9

Printed in the United States of America

Printing *(last digit):* 9 8 7 6 5 4 3 2 1

Contents

FOR PHIL MASON

Introduction

Traditionally, the fourth earl of Sandwich (1718–1792) is credited with creating the sandwich. The story is told that the earl was so interested in card playing that he would not leave the card table even to eat. Therefore he instructed a servant to serve him slices of meat between slices of bread so that he could eat while continuing the game. Whether or not the earl, in fact, invented the sandwich, it obviously bears his name. People probably have been eating meats and cheeses between slices of bread since the invention of bread itself.

Whoever is responsible, sandwiches are unquestionably popular. They provide a quick meal that can be hearty enough to satisfy a true trencherman. (Originally a trencher was a slice of bread used as a plate in the Middle Ages.) Or, they can be light and delicate enough to satisfy the most discriminating eater at tea. Although Americans love sandwiches without equal, other countries have their favorite versions. The Scandinavians, especially the Danes, lunch regularly on open-faced sandwiches that are works of art. In France, they produce delicate canapes as well as whole loaf sandwiches that make impressive meals. The English have their delicate tea sandwiches as well as simple bread and cheese. In the past, it was common for Chinese peasants to take steamed wheat buns, filled with garlic cloves, into the fields for lunch. Wealthier Chinese would eat the same buns filled with ground pork and spices as a between-meal snack.

Sandwiches are a delicious, simple way to increase your sales and profits. Whether in a diner, a cafeteria, or a four-star restaurant, the intelligent chef will provide sandwiches for diners who want light, savory meals served quickly. Carefully selected sandwiches can be used to enhance most menus. For instance, the diner that offers different types of sandwiches, such as those made with pita bread or interesting and tasteful fillings, will have an edge over those that produce mundane egg salad or tasteless tuna. The cafeteria that serves the same people every day can spark interest by offering some of the more exotic sandwiches suggested here, such as open-faced sandwiches. The fine dining room has the opportunity to offer a variety of canapes as appetizers or to complement cocktails. Restaurants with supper menus will find that late evening guests are partial to such offerings as club sandwiches or croque-monsieur.

We have assumed that the average kitchen worker can produce an acceptable roast beef, turkey, tuna, or egg salad sandwich, garnished perhaps with a slice of tomato and a leaf or two of lettuce. Therefore, this book presents different suggestions for sandwiches, using ordinary ingredients, to introduce more excitement into your menus and increase sales on your books.

The quality of a sandwich stands or falls on the quality of the bread. The best fillings are worthless if the bread is not the best. Tasteless, spongy breads must be rejected. Hard breads or rolls (French, Italian, submarine, hero, or grinder) should have a crisp crust with a chewy yet tender crumb. Whole wheat, rye, and pumpernickel should have a full, natural flavor with a firm crumb. Depending on the variety, the crust may be soft or crisp. If you are using some of the imported German pumpernickels or volkenbrots, the crumb may even be quite solid. Pita or Syrian bread should be thin, pliable, and of good flavor. It should also split open easily and not be thick and gummy. American or white bread should have a firm, even texture with a full flavor. Providing quality breads is not that much more expensive, and it makes good sense, resulting in increased sales and the ability to charge accordingly. The capable chef will locate a supplier of the best quality breads, according to the needs of the kitchen, or make sure that the in-house baker provides only the best.

Although almost any food can be used as a sandwich filling, some obviously are more appropriate than others. There are still New Englanders who feel that nothing is as tasty as a baked bean sandwich; and children will continue to make up concoctions of peanut butter, banana, pickles, and other disparately flavored foods to shock their parents. However, a chef must select a filling appropriate to the bread and the type of sandwich. And the heartier the filling, the thicker the bread. Inch-thick slabs of rye bread with a thinly sliced cucumber filling would be as ridiculous as paper-thin slices of white bread with thick slices of corned beef. There should be a complementary relationship between the type and amount of filling and the type and thickness of bread. Hearty sandwiches can be made with chunks of cubed chicken, but thin tea sandwiches should be made with correspondingly thin slices of chicken breast.

In addition to using carefully selected, delicious fillings with good quality breads, a fine sandwich must *look* inviting. All too often, kitchen workers throw the ingredients onto a slice of bread, put another slice on top, and call it a sandwich. Sandwiches should be neat. Depending on the filling and type of sandwich, the crusts may or may not be trimmed. The ingredients should fit on the bread to all the edges without spilling messily over the sides. Sandwiches should be cut so that guests can pick them up without fear of spilling the contents. Overfilled sandwiches that lose their filling are just as irritating, if not more so, as sandwiches with so little filling that the customers cannot identify the contents.

Sandwiches with moist fillings should be prepared just before serving so they will not become limp and soggy. If the sandwiches must be made ahead, it may be necessary to use a different filling. For a large tea or picnic, when sandwiches must be prepared ahead, it is important to use drier fillings and to protect the bread from getting soggy by buttering generously. Arrange the sandwiches on trays, cover them with waxed paper, and place towels wrung out in cold water over them to keep them fresh in the refrigerator for several hours. Toast should be made to order or it becomes soggy and chewy. The best toast is made in the oven. It is dry and crisp rather than brown on the exterior and still moist inside. Hot sandwiches are served on heated plates; cold sandwiches are served on chilled plates. Never serve a cold sandwich on a plate hot from the dishwasher.

Remember, the restaurant or dining room that receives praise for its sandwiches, and gets repeat business and the corresponding increase in sales, is the one that takes the extra effort to use quality ingredients and serve them as attractively as possible.

Although it is not always practiced, one of the first laws of cookery is that nothing is absolute. This applies especially to sandwiches. If a recipe calls for rye bread and you have only French bread, go ahead and use it. Be inventive with the fillings also. Many sandwiches can be served in pita bread, or a combination of fillings can be used in the large composed sandwiches in Chapter 4. Many fillings can also be used inside a hollowed-out French roll (see the recipe for Saucisson en Croute in Chapter 2). The variations are practically limitless.

Chapter 1

Cold Sandwiches

The finest ingredients are required to make the best sandwiches. However, even the best of ingredients can be destroyed by slovenly work practices. The meat for sandwiches should be cut into thin slices, with the possible exception of liverwurst. There is usually more flavor in a number of paper-thin slices of meat than in one thick chunk. Taste for yourself a sandwich of thin slices of ham between two very thin slices of buttered bread and compare to a sandwich of bread and ham slices cut almost equally thick.

Egg and Anchovy Sandwich with Shrimp

3 hard-cooked eggs
4 anchovy fillets, drained and chopped
1/4 cup butter, softened
1/2 teaspoon minced onion
1 tablespoon mayonnaise
1 teaspoon Dijon mustard
  salt and pepper to taste
12 slices white bread, buttered
  sprigs of watercress
12 large shrimp

In a bowl, mash the eggs, anchovy fillets, butter, and onion to a paste. Stir in the mayonnaise, mustard, salt, and pepper.

Spread on half the bread slices and sprinkle with sprigs of watercress. Cut shrimp in half along the back and place on the egg mixture. Cover with remaining bread slices.

Yields 6 sandwiches.

A thin coating of butter spread on the bread makes almost any sandwich taste better. In addition, the butter serves as a shield to prevent juices from seeping into the bread and making the sandwich soggy. Dressings and condiments, such as mayonnaise and ketchup, should be added to sandwiches at the customer's direction, except for those made with fillings bound with mayonnaise.

For interest and variety, where possible, offer guests a selection of breads and rolls and let them make their own choice. Restaurants already offering salad bars should consider setting up sandwich bars, allowing the luncheon crowd to build their own sandwiches.

Smoked Salmon and Caviar Sandwich

12 slices pumpernickel
1/2 cup russian dressing
1/4 pound smoked salmon, thinly sliced
1/2 cup red caviar
1/4 cup minced onion

Spread pumpernickel slices with russian dressing. Place a layer of salmon on half the slices and spread with caviar. Sprinkle with onion and cover with remaining bread slices.

Yields 6 sandwiches.

Sardine and Egg Sandwich

6 skinless and boneless sardines

3 hard-cooked eggs, chopped

3 tablespoons butter

1 teaspoon grated lemon rind

1/2 teaspoon minced onion

　lemon juice to taste

　salt and pepper to taste

12 slices Westphalian pumper-
　nickel

In a processor, combine the sardines, eggs, butter, lemon rind, and onion. Process with the plastic blade into a coarse mixture. Season with lemon juice, salt, and pepper.

Yields 6 sandwiches.

Cucumber and Shrimp Sandwich

1 cucumber, thinly sliced

1/2 cup tarragon vinegar

1 tablespoon sugar

12 slices white toast

2 tablespoons tartar sauce

1/2 pound tiny shrimp, cooked

In a bowl, combine the cucumber, vinegar, and sugar. Toss well and marinate for 1 hour or longer.

Spread toast slices with tartar sauce. Arrange shrimp on half of the toast slices and cover with well-drained cucumber slices. Cover with remaining slices, tartar sauce side down.

Yields 6 sandwiches.

Tuna and Egg Filling for Pita Sandwich

2 7-ounce cans flaked tuna
2 hard-cooked eggs, chopped
1/4 cup lemon juice
1/4 cup chopped ripe olives
1/4 teaspoon thyme
   salt and pepper to taste
6 small pita loaves
1 cup shredded lettuce

In a bowl, combine the tuna, eggs, lemon juice, olives, thyme, salt, and pepper. Mix well.

Cut pita loaves in half crosswise. Open the halves and insert a layer of lettuce. Add the tuna mixture.

Yields 6 sandwiches.

Tuna and Watercress Sandwich

1 7-ounce can tuna, drained and flaked
1 teaspoon lemon juice
1 teaspoon grated lemon rind
1/2 cup chopped watercress
   mayonnaise to taste
8 slices white bread, buttered

In a bowl, combine the tuna, lemon juice, and rind. Mix well. Add the watercress and fold in just enough mayonnaise to bind.

Spread the mixture on half of the slices and cover with remaining slices. Trim crusts if desired.

Yields 4 sandwiches.

Chicken and Chutney Sandwich

1/2 cup minced chicken
1/2 cup minced chutney
1/2 cup cream cheese
1/4 cup chopped salted cashews
12 slices whole wheat bread, buttered

In a bowl, combine the chicken, chutney, cheese, and nuts. Mix well. Spread on buttered bread.

Yields 6 sandwiches.

Curried Chicken Sandwich

2 cups diced chicken
1/2 cup diced celery
1/2 cup diced tart apple
1/3 cup chopped seedless grapes
1/4 cup mayonnaise
1/2 teaspoon salt
1-1/2 teaspoons curry powder
2 teaspoons lemon juice
12 slices buttered bread or 6 French rolls, split and buttered

In a bowl, combine the chicken, celery, apple, grapes, mayonnaise, salt, curry powder, and lemon juice. Mix gently.

Yields 6 sandwiches.

Chicken, or Pork, and Pepper Sandwich

12 slices white bread or toast
    mayonnaise
12 slices chicken, turkey, or roast pork

12 roasted sweet red peppers
12 leaves Belgian endive
3/4 cup sliced, pitted Greek olives

Spread bread slices with mayonnaise. Put two pieces of meat on half of the slices and cover with peppers, endive, and olives. Cover with remaining bread slices.

Yields 6 sandwiches.

Boeuf d'Auvergne

Beef and Roquefort Sandwich

12 slices French bread, buttered
6 tablespoons bleu d'Auvergne or Roquefort cheese
2 pounds rare roast beef, thinly sliced
    black pepper to taste
6 thin slices Bermuda onion

Spread half of the bread slices with Roquefort. Arrange the beef on top. Season with pepper and top with onion slices. Cover with remaining bread slices.

Yields 6 sandwiches.

1 *Cold Sandwiches*

Roast Beef and Chevre Cheese Sandwich

6 Kaiser rolls, buttered
12 slices rare roast beef
6 thin slices chevre cheese
6 tomato slices
12 slices crisp bacon
   black pepper to taste

Arrange the bottoms of the rolls on a board and put beef slices on them. Top with slices of cheese, tomato, and bacon.

Sprinkle each sandwich generously with pepper and cover with tops of the rolls.

Yields 6 sandwiches.

Minced Cold Roast Beef Sandwich

1/2 pound rare roast beef, minced
2 tablespoons minced onion
1 tablespoon horseradish, or to taste
   salt and pepper to taste
   mayonnaise
12 slices Russian rye or white bread, buttered

In a bowl, combine the beef, onion, horseradish, salt, and pepper. Add just enough mayonnaise to bind.

Yields 6 sandwiches.

Roast Beef and Mustard Roll

2 cups minced, very rare roast beef
1 tablespoon minced celery leaves
1 teaspoon Dijon mustard
1 teaspoon onion juice
1 teaspoon Worcestershire sauce
   salt and pepper to taste
   pinch of sugar
6 French rolls, split and buttered

In a bowl, combine the beef, celery leaves, mustard, onion juice, Worcestershire, salt, pepper, and sugar. Mix lightly.

Yields 6 sandwiches.

Pepitos

1 tomato, peeled, seeded, and chopped
1/4 cup minced onion
1/4 cup minced Serrano chilies
1/2 pound flank steak
2 tablespoons butter
6 whole wheat rolls or pita loaves
salt and pepper to taste

In a bowl, combine the tomato, onion, and chilies. Mix well and marinate for at least 30 minutes.

Cut the steak into 1/4-inch thick slices. In a large skillet, saute the steak in butter until browned but still rare. Set aside.

Split the rolls and dip into the pan juices. (If using pita pockets, pour some of the juices inside.) Arrange steak slices on bottoms of rolls and place the tomato mixture on top. Season with salt and pepper and cover with roll tops.

Yields 6 sandwiches.

Corned Beef Sandwich

2 tablespoons butter
1 tablespoon mustard
12 slices bauernbrot
1/2 pound warm corned beef, thinly sliced
12 tomato slices
6 lettuce leaves

In a bowl, combine the butter and mustard and spread on the bread.

Arrange slices of corned beef, tomato, and lettuce on half the bread slices and cover with remaining slices.

Yields 6 sandwiches.

*1*Cold Sandwiches

Minced Veal Sandwich

2 tablespoons anchovy butter
12 thin slices white bread
3/4 cup minced, cooked veal
mayonnaise to taste

Spread anchovy butter on bread slices.

Combine the veal with enough mayonnaise to bind and use to make sandwiches.

Yields 6 sandwiches.

Lamb in Pita Bread with Yogurt Sauce

1 cup yogurt
1 tablespoon lemon juice
1 tablespoon minced mint
1 garlic clove, minced
salt and pepper to taste
4 pita loaves
1/2 pound cooked lamb, sliced
2 tomatoes, thinly sliced
1/2 cucumber, thinly sliced
1 red onion, thinly sliced
minced parsley

In a bowl, combine the yogurt, lemon juice, mint, garlic, salt, and pepper.

Split the loaves open on one edge, about 1/4 of the diameter. Fill the pocket with layers of lamb, tomato, cucumber, and onion.

Pour 1/4 of the sauce into each and sprinkle with parsley.

Yields 4 sandwiches.

Pork and Apple Sandwich

12 thin slices white or whole wheat bread, buttered
3/4 cup thick apple sauce
salt and pepper to taste
12 slices roast pork

Spread half the bread slices with apple sauce and arrange pork slices on top. Season with salt and pepper and cover with remaining bread slices.

Yields 6 sandwiches.

Turkey, Ham, and Egg Sandwich

12 slices caraway rye bread
4 tablespoons russian dressing
6 slices turkey
6 slices baked ham
2 tomatoes, thinly sliced
2 hard-cooked eggs, thinly sliced
6 lettuce leaves, preferably romaine

Spread bread with russian dressing. On half the slices layer the turkey, ham, tomato, and egg slices. Arrange lettuce neatly on top and cover with remaining bread slices.
Yields 6 sandwiches.

Ham Filling for Pita Bread

1 pound ham, in 1/4-inch cubes
mustard mayonnaise
1/2 cup chopped dill pickles
6 pita loaves

In a bowl, combine the ham with just enough mayonnaise to bind. Fold in the pickles and mix well. Fill the pita pockets.
Yields 6 sandwiches.

Ham Paste Sandwich

1-1/2 cups ground lean ham
4 tablespoons butter, softened
Dijon mustard to taste
heavy cream
12 very thin slices rye bread
mayonnaise

In a bowl, combine the ham, butter, and mustard. Add just enough heavy cream to make a smooth paste.
Spread bread slices with a thin layer of mayonnaise. Spread ham on half the slices and cover with remaining bread slices. Cut into shapes as desired, removing the crusts.
Yields 6 sandwiches.

1 Cold Sandwiches

Tongue Sandwich

2 cups ground cooked tongue

1/2 cup mayonnaise

1/2 cup minced dill pickle

2 tablespoons minced onion

2 teaspoons Dijon mustard

1-1/2 teaspoons Worcestershire sauce

1 teaspoon tomato paste

salt and pepper to taste

12 slices white or rye bread

In a bowl, combine the tongue, mayonnaise, pickle, onion, mustard, Worcestershire, tomato paste, salt, and pepper.

Yields 6 sandwiches.

Tongue and Roquefort Sandwich

1-1/2 cups minced, cooked smoked tongue

1/3 cup crumbled Roquefort cheese

vinaigrette dressing

12 slices rye bread, buttered

In a bowl, combine the tongue, Roquefort, and enough vinaigrette to moisten.

Yields 6 sandwiches.

Tongue and Horseradish Sandwich

6 thin slices whole wheat bread

6 thin slices white bread

3 ounces cream cheese, softened

salt and pepper to taste

6 tablespoons butter

1 tablespoon grated horseradish

12 thin slices tongue

Arrange bread slices on a flat surface.

Cream the cheese and season with salt and pepper. Spread on whole wheat bread.

Cream the butter and horseradish and spread on white bread. Arrange tongue slices on the cream cheese and top with buttered white bread.

Yields 6 sandwiches.

Tongue and Egg Sandwich

1/2 pound boiled tongue, minced

2 hard-cooked eggs, mashed

1 tablespoon Dijon mustard

salt and cayenne pepper to taste

2 to 3 tablespoons cream

12 slices white or whole wheat bread, buttered

In a processor, combine the tongue, eggs, mustard, salt, and cayenne. Puree, adding enough cream to make a smooth spreadable mixture.

Yields 6 sandwiches.

Chicken Liver Sandwich

1/2 pound chicken livers

1 cup chopped mushrooms

4 tablespoons butter

2/3 cup chopped red pepper

6 tablespoons minced onion

2 tablespoons mayonnaise

salt and pepper to taste

6 French rolls, split and buttered

In a skillet, saute the livers and mushrooms in butter until the livers are lightly browned, but still pink inside.

Place liver mixture in a blender or processor with the red pepper and onion. Puree, adding the mayonnaise, salt, and pepper. Chill 1 hour.

Yields 6 sandwiches.

Liverwurst Sandwich

1 pound liverwurst, diced

1/2 cup minced scallions

1/2 cup shredded lettuce

2 teaspoons Dijon mustard

mayonnaise

6 slices white bread, buttered

6 slices whole wheat bread, buttered

In a bowl, combine the liverwurst, scallions, lettuce, mustard, and just enough mayonnaise to bind. Stir gently.

Assemble sandwiches using one slice white and one slice whole wheat bread.

Yields 6 sandwiches.

Avocado and Bacon Sandwich

2 ripe avocados

1 teaspoon lemon or lime juice

1/2 teaspoon grated onion

1/2 teaspoon Worcestershire sauce
   salt and pepper to taste

12 slices whole wheat bread, toasted

12 strips crisp bacon

In a bowl, mash the avocado and stir in lemon juice, onion, Worcestershire, salt, and pepper.

Spread on half the toast slices and top each with two strips of bacon. Cover with remaining toast slices.

Yields 6 sandwiches.

Bacon and Pimiento Sandwich

24 slices crisp bacon, crumbled

1-1/2 cups drained, chopped pimiento

6 tablespoons mayonnaise
   salt and pepper to taste

12 slices whole wheat bread, buttered

In a bowl, combine the bacon, pimiento, mayonnaise, salt, and pepper.

Yields 6 sandwiches.

Chapter 2

Hot Sandwiches

Hot sandwiches are perhaps even more popular than cold ones. They provide wonderful opportunities for the chef to be inventive. A little imagination can result in spectacular combinations. This chapter provides some delicious examples that may encourage you to create your own signature sandwich.

Without question, the most popular hot sandwich in the United States, if not the world, is the hamburger. Both broiled and sauteed versions are included here, but you should consider developing some interesting versions of your own.

Horseradish Cheese Croute

6 thin slices white bread
4 tablespoons butter
3/4 cup grated Gruyere cheese
3/4 cup grated Parmesan cheese
3 tablespoons heavy cream
1 tablespoon grated horseradish
 tarragon vinegar to taste
 paprika

Preheat oven to 400° F.

Saute bread slices in butter until golden on both sides.

In a bowl, combine the cheeses, cream, horseradish, and vinegar. Spread evenly on the toasts. Bake for 5 minutes. Sprinkle with paprika.

Yields 6 sandwiches.

By adding herbs to the meat, or using different cheeses, you can improve the image of your dining room, along with your profit picture.

Because hot sandwiches are often served open and sauced, it is not only acceptable but also proper to serve them with the contents spreading over the top. However, your presentation still must look appetizing. Such sandwiches must be served with a knife and fork.

Croute du Lion d'Or

2 shallots, minced
2 tablespoons butter
3/4 pound mushrooms, minced
1 cup minced ham
2/3 cup heavy cream
1 teaspoon curry powder
  salt
6 slices toast, crusts removed
1/2 cup Mousseline sauce

Preheat broiler.

In a skillet, saute shallots in butter until soft. Add the mushrooms and cook over moderate heat until liquid has evaporated. Stir in the ham, cream, curry powder, and salt and simmer 3 minutes.

Spread toast slices with the mixture and place on a baking sheet. Spoon Mousseline over each toast and brown under the broiler.

Yields 6 sandwiches.

Note: To make Mousseline sauce, fold 2 tablespoons of whipped cream into 6 tablespoons Hollandaise sauce.

Crab and Mushroom French Roll

1 cup crabmeat

1/2 pound mushrooms, minced

3/4 cup mayonnaise

4 tablespoons grated Parmesan cheese

1 tablespoon minced parsley

1 teaspoon lemon juice

1/8 teaspoon rosemary

1/8 teaspoon thyme

1/8 teaspoon sage

6 French or Kaiser rolls

butter

6 tablespoons slivered toasted almonds

Preheat oven to 350° F.

In a bowl, combine the crabmeat, mushrooms, mayonnaise, cheese, parsley, lemon juice, rosemary, thyme, and sage.

Split rolls in half and toast. Spread bottoms of rolls with butter and then with crab mixture. Sprinkle almonds on top and cover with tops of the rolls.

Wrap each roll in foil and heat for 20 minutes, or wrap in plastic wrap and heat in microwave for 1 minute.

Yields 6 sandwiches.

Soft-Shelled Crab Sandwich

3/4 cup clarified butter

2 garlic cloves, thinly sliced

6 slices white bread

6 soft-shelled crabs

flour

6 lettuce leaves

6 tablespoons Remoulade sauce (see Chapter 11)

In a skillet, heat butter and garlic until garlic is golden. Discard the garlic. Saute the bread on both sides in the butter and drain on paper toweling.

Dredge crabs in flour and saute in the butter, adding more if needed, until golden on both sides.

Arrange lettuce on toasts and put a crab on top. Garnish with Remoulade sauce.

Yields 6 sandwiches.

Crabmeat Lorenzo

1 garlic clove, minced
1/4 cup butter
1/3 cup minced scallions
1/4 cup minced green pepper
2 teaspoons flour
1/2 cup milk
1 pound crabmeat, flaked
1/2 cup stale bread crumbs
1/4 cup dry sherry
salt and pepper to taste
6 5-inch toast rounds
12 anchovy fillets
6 tablespoons grated Parmesan cheese

Preheat broiler.

In a skillet, saute the garlic in butter for 3 minutes. Add scallions and peppers and simmer, stirring, for 10 minutes, or until soft but not brown. Stir in flour and cook, stirring, for 1 minute. Stir in milk and cook, stirring, until thickened. Stir in crabmeat, bread crumbs, sherry, salt, and pepper.

Mound the mixture on toast rounds. Arrange anchovy fillets on top and sprinkle with cheese. Broil until golden.

Yields 6 sandwiches.

Broiled Crabmeat Rounds

6 slices white bread, toasted
1 cup crabmeat
2 hard-cooked eggs, minced
1/4 cup minced dill pickle
1/4 cup mayonnaise
2 to 3 tablespoons lemon juice
salt and pepper to taste
Tabasco sauce to taste
butter
6 tomato slices
6 tablespoons grated Parmesan cheese
butter

Preheat oven to 400° F.

Cut bread into large or small rounds, if desired.

In a bowl, combine the crabmeat, eggs, pickles, mayonnaise, lemon juice, salt, pepper, and Tabasco.

Spread toasts with butter and then with crabmeat mixture. Top each with a tomato slice and season with salt and pepper. Sprinkle with cheese and dot with butter. Bake for 10 minutes or until cheese is melted.

Yields 6 sandwiches.

Open-Faced Flounder Sandwich

8 slices buttered toast, crusts removed
1 pound flounder fillets, cooked
7 teaspoons tartar sauce
salt and pepper to taste
6 thin slices tomato
12 tablespoons grated Gruyere cheese

Preheat broiler.

Flake the cooked fish and fold in tartar sauce, salt, and pepper. Spread on the toast slices and top with tomato and cheese. Broil until the cheese is bubbly.

Yields 6 sandwiches.

Grilled Lobster Sandwich Aurora

1/2 cup Bechamel sauce
1-1/2 teaspoons tomato paste
1 teaspoon lemon juice
1-1/2 cups cooked lobster, diced
6 slices white bread, crusts removed
6 tablespoons grated Gruyere cheese

Preheat broiler.

Reduce Bechamel to 1/3 cup and mix in tomato paste and lemon juice. Fold in the lobster.

Toast the bread slices on one side. Spread untoasted sides with lobster mixture and sprinkle with cheese. Broil until lightly browned.

Yields 6 sandwiches.

Brandied Lobster Sandwich

3/4 cup thick Bechamel sauce
1 tablespoon tomato paste
2 tablespoons cognac
2 tablespoons minced parsley
1/2 teaspoon salt
pinch of grated nutmeg
1/4 teaspoon minced tarragon
pepper to taste
1 cup cooked lobster, diced
6 slices white bread, crusts removed
butter
1/4 cup grated Gruyere cheese

Preheat broiler.

Heat Bechamel and stir in the tomato paste, cognac, parsley, salt, nutmeg, tarragon, and pepper. Fold in the lobster and heat through.

Toast bread on one side. Butter untoasted side. Spread with lobster mixture and sprinkle with cheese. Broil until cheese is bubbly and lightly browned.

Yields 6 sandwiches.

Oyster Sandwich

6 slices rye bread
2 tablespoons butter
2 teaspoons anchovy paste
24 oysters, shucked and drained
salt and pepper to taste
12 slices Monterey Jack cheese

Preheat oven to 400°F.

Butter bread on one side and place, buttered side down, on a baking sheet. Spread anchovy paste on unbuttered side. Place four oysters on each slice and season with salt and pepper. Arrange cheese on the oysters.

Bake for 10 minutes. Glaze under the broiler.

Yields 6 sandwiches.

Salmon Souffle Sandwich

12 slices tomato
6 slices buttered toast
salt and pepper to taste
1-1/2 cups flaked, cooked salmon
1-1/2 cups grated sharp cheddar cheese
4 eggs, separated
2 teaspoons Worcestershire sauce
2 teaspoons Dijon mustard
1/4 teaspoon paprika

Preheat oven to 350°F.

Arrange two tomato slices on each piece of toast and season with salt and pepper. Place salmon on top. Arrange on lightly buttered baking sheet.

In a bowl, combine cheese, egg yolks, Worcestershire, mustard, paprika, salt, and pepper.

Beat egg whites with a pinch of salt until stiff but not dry. Fold into the cheese mixture and spread over salmon. Bake for 15 minutes or until puffed and golden.

Yields 6 sandwiches.

2 Hot
Sandwiches

Mary Garden Sandwich

6 slices white bread

3 small chicken breasts, thinly sliced

12 mushroom caps, sliced

butter

12 asparagus tips, cooked

1-1/2 cups Mornay sauce

parsley sprigs

Preheat broiler.

Arrange bread on heatproof serving plates. Place chicken slices on top.

Saute the mushrooms in butter until tender and place on the chicken. Arrange half the asparagus next to the mushrooms.

Coat sandwiches with sauce and glaze under the broiler. Garnish with remaining asparagus and parsley.

Yields 6 sandwiches.

Chicken and Gherkin Sandwich

6 slices rye bread

butter

thin slices cooked chicken

salt and pepper to taste

1 tablespoon thinly sliced gherkin

3 tablespoons grated mozzarella cheese

Preheat oven to 400° F.

Toast bread on one side and lightly butter untoasted side. Arrange chicken slices on untoasted side and season with salt and pepper.

Arrange gherkin slices on chicken and sprinkle with cheese. Bake for 10 minutes or until lightly browned.

Yields 6 sandwiches.

Puffed Chicken Sandwich

1-2/3 cups diced cooked chicken
1/2 cup chopped celery
1/3 cup mayonnaise
1-1/2 tablespoons lemon juice
   salt and pepper to taste
6 slices whole wheat bread
3 egg whites
3/4 cup grated cheddar or
   Parmesan cheese

Preheat oven to 450° F.

In a bowl, combine the chicken, celery, mayonnaise, lemon juice, salt, and pepper.

Toast bread on one side and lightly butter untoasted side. Spread chicken mixture on untoasted side.

Beat the egg whites with a pinch of salt until stiff but not dry. Fold in cheese and spread on top of chicken. Bake until puffed and golden, about 10 minutes.

Yields 6 sandwiches.

Broiled Chicken Sandwich

1-1/2 cups diced cooked chicken
6 tablespoons butter, softened
1/4 cup heavy cream
1 tablespoon lemon juice
1/2 teaspoon ground thyme
   salt and pepper to taste
6 slices buttered toast
   grated Parmesan cheese

Preheat broiler.

In a bowl, combine the chicken and butter. Fold in cream, lemon juice, thyme, salt, and pepper. Spread buttered side of toast with chicken mixture and sprinkle with grated cheese. Glaze under the broiler.

Yields 6 sandwiches.

2 *Hot Sandwiches*

Devonshire Sandwich

18 slices bacon

3/4 cup bacon fat

1 cup flour

1 quart milk

1 pound sharp cheddar cheese, grated

2 teaspoons dry mustard

salt to taste

pinch of sage

6 slices toast

18 thin slices chicken or turkey

1/4 cup grated Parmesan cheese

Preheat oven to 350° F.

Cook bacon until crisp. Drain and reserve fat. Heat bacon fat, stir in flour, and cook, stirring, for 3 minutes. Stir in the milk and cook, stirring, until thick and smooth. Stir in the cheddar cheese and mustard and cook, stirring, until cheese is melted. Season with salt and sage.

Place toast on heatproof serving plates and arrange bacon slices on top. Place chicken slices on bacon and coat generously with sauce.

Sprinkle grated Parmesan over top and bake until hot and bubbly.

Glaze under broiler, if desired.

Yields 6 sandwiches.

Bacon and Turkey Sandwich

6 slices rye bread, toasted

mayonnaise to taste

6 thin slices turkey

12 slices crisp bacon

6 1/2-inch thick slices tomato

6 slices Gruyere cheese

Preheat oven to 400° F.

Spread toast with mayonnaise and layer turkey, bacon, tomato, and cheese on top.

Bake for 10 minutes, or until cheese is melted.

Yields 6 sandwiches.

Greek Country
Salad Loaf
(See page 51.)

**Roquefort-Filled
Hamburger with
Sauce Pancho**
(See page 24.)

**Chicken Liver and
Apple Sandwich**
(See page 90.)

Roast Beef and Chevre Cheese Sandwich
(See page 6.)

Sausage and Cheese Pain Perdu
(See page 103.)

Sardine and Egg Sandwich
(See page 3.)

Shrimp Canapes
(See page 94.)

Milwaukee Sandwich
(See page 105.)

Turkey Rarebit Sandwich

3 tablespoons butter
3 tablespoons flour
1-1/2 cups cubed cheddar cheese
1/4 teaspoon dry mustard
milk
8 slices white bread, toasted
1/2 pound turkey, thinly sliced
8 slices tomato
16 slices crisp bacon

Preheat broiler.

In a saucepan, melt the butter over medium heat and stir in flour. Stir in the cheese and cook, stirring, until cheese is melted. Stir in the mustard and enough milk to thin the sauce so that it lightly coats the back of a spoon. Keep warm.

Place toast slices on heatproof plates and arrange turkey slices on top. Coat with sauce.

Glaze under the broiler. Garnish with tomato slices and bacon strips.

Yields 8 sandwiches.

Open-Faced Stromboli Sandwich

6 1/2-inch thick slices French bread, toasted
6 1/2-inch thick slices tenderloin
butter
6 thin slices ham
6 thin slices mozzarella cheese
6 pitted ripe olives

Preheat broiler.

Arrange toast slices on a baking sheet.

In a skillet, saute tenderloin in butter, keeping it rare. Place the tenderloin slices on toast and top with ham and cheese. Broil until cheese begins to melt.

Garnish each with a ripe olive.

Yields 6 sandwiches.

2 Hot Sandwiches

Roquefort-Filled Hamburger with Sauce Pancho

      3/4 cup ketchup
        6 tablespoons chili sauce
        6 tablespoons mayonnaise
        2 tablespoons pineapple juice
    2-1/4 teaspoons wine vinegar
    2-1/4 teaspoons dry mustard
    1-1/2 teaspoons Worcestershire
          sauce
      3/4 teaspoon horseradish
      1/4 teaspoon ground ginger
          Tabasco sauce to taste
        1 small onion, minced
        2 tablespoons olive oil
        1 garlic clove, minced
        2 pounds ground beef
        2 eggs
        1 tablespoon minced parsley
          salt and pepper to taste
        6 tablespoons crumbled
          Roquefort cheese
        2 tablespoons butter, softened
        2 tablespoons cognac
        6 French bread rolls

Preheat broiler.

In a bowl, combine the ketchup, chili sauce, mayonnaise, pineapple juice, vinegar, mustard, Worcestershire, horseradish, ginger, and Tabasco. Mix well and refrigerate for 2 hours.

In a small skillet, saute the onion in oil until soft. Add garlic and cook until it just begins to brown.

In a bowl, combine the beef, eggs, parsley, onion mixture, salt, and pepper. Shape into 6 patties and make a depression in the center of each.

Combine the Roquefort, butter, and cognac and divide among the patties. Press edges of the meat around cheese mixture to enclose it.

Broil patties until done. Serve on French rolls and pass the sauce.

Yields 6 sandwiches.

Boeuf Hache aux Chevre et Poivre

Hamburger with Goat Cheese and Pepper

3 pounds ground beef
    freshly cracked pepper
    coarse salt
2/3 cup cognac
    butter
6 club rolls, split and toasted
6 ounces chevre cheese

Shape the meat into six patties. Press cracked pepper into both sides of patties.

In a heavy iron skillet, sprinkled generously with salt, saute patties to the desired degree of doneness. Remove patties from the pan and pour off excess salt. Add the cognac to pan and cook, stirring, until reduced to 2 tablespoons.

Butter the rolls and arrange burgers on top. Pour on the pan juices. Garnish each burger with a slice of chevre.

Yields 6 sandwiches.

Boeuf Hache a Cheval

Hamburger with Fried Eggs

 6 bread rounds, sauteed in butter
 6 rare hamburgers
 6 fried eggs
12 anchovy fillets

Arrange the hamburgers on toast rounds. Place eggs on top and garnish with anchovy fillets.

Yields 6 sandwiches.

2 Hot Sandwiches

Hamburger Provencal

3 pounds ground beef

3 garlic cloves, minced
   olive oil

6 hamburger rolls

6 slices eggplant, sauteed

1/2 cup tomato coulis (see
   Chapter 11)

Combine the beef and garlic and shape into six hamburgers. Saute in olive oil until cooked to desired degree.

Arrange hamburgers on bottom halves of hamburger rolls. Arrange eggplant slices on remaining halves and garnish with tomato coulis.

Yields 6 sandwiches.

Reuben Sandwich

6 large slices dark rye, toasted
   butter

6 tablespoons russian dressing

1-1/2 pounds corned beef, thinly
   sliced

1 pound sauerkraut, rinsed and
   drained

6 large slices Gruyere cheese

Preheat oven to 400° F.

Spread toast with butter and then with russian dressing. Arrange corned beef on the toast and top with sauerkraut and cheese.

Bake for 5 to 7 minutes, or until sandwiches are heated and cheese has started to melt.

Yields 6 sandwiches.

Lamb Sandwich

6 slices firm white bread

2 tablespoons mustard butter

1-1/2 pounds hot roast lamb, thinly
   sliced
   mint sprigs

Spread bread with mustard butter and arrange lamb slices on top. Garnish with mint.

Yields 6 sandwiches.

Panini Rustici
Rustic Bread

- 1 pound ricotta cheese
- 2 eggs
- 1/2 teaspoon salt
- 1/2 pound mozzarella cheese, diced
- 1/4 pound salami, diced
- 1/4 pound prosciutto, diced
- 1/4 pound mortadella, diced
- 6 Italian rolls, halved
- 1/2 cup grated Parmesan cheese
  pepper to taste
- 4 tablespoons butter

Preheat oven to 350°F.

In a bowl, combine the ricotta, eggs, salt, mozzarella, salami, prosciutto, and mortadella. Mix well and spread on halved rolls. Sprinkle with Parmesan and pepper. Dot with butter.

Bake 10 to 15 minutes or until heated thoroughly. If desired, run under the broiler to brown tops.

Yields 6 sandwiches.

Crostini Caldo d'Andrea
Hot Toasts Andrea

- 6 slices mozzarella cheese
- 2 teaspoons capers, minced
- 4 ounces anchovies, soaked in milk
- 6 mushrooms, thinly sliced
- 2 tablespoons minced parsley
- 1 teaspoon crumbled dried basil
- 6 slices Gruyere cheese
- 3 tomatoes, thinly sliced
- 6 tablespoons grated Parmesan cheese
- 6 slices prosciutto
- 6 slices Italian bread, toasted
  olive oil
  pepper

Preheat oven to 400°F.

Layer mozzarella, capers, drained anchovies, mushrooms, parsley, basil, Gruyere, tomatoes, Parmesan, and prosciutto on toast. Brush with oil and sprinkle with pepper.

Bake until cheese melts slightly.

Yields 6 sandwiches.

Croute au Reblochon

Prosciutto and Reblochon Sandwich

6 slices whole wheat bread, crusts removed
2 tablespoons butter
6 thin slices prosciutto
6 1/4-inch thick slices Reblochon cheese
6 tablespoons bread crumbs
3 tablespoons minced parsley
6 tablespoons heavy cream
   salt and pepper to taste

Preheat oven to 375° F.

Toast bread lightly on both sides. Spread with butter and top with prosciutto and Reblochon. Place on a baking sheet.

Combine bread crumbs, parsley, cream, salt, and pepper. Spread over each sandwich. Bake until heated and the cheese begins to soften, but not run.

Yields 6 sandwiches.

Cheese and Mushroom Sandwich

2/3 cup duxelles (see Chapter 11)
   1 cup Bechamel sauce
   1 small tomato, peeled, seeded, and chopped
   1 small garlic clove, minced
      salt and pepper to taste
   8 thin slices white bread, toasted
   8 thin slices ham
      grated Gruyere or Parmesan cheese

Preheat broiler.

Combine the duxelles, Bechamel, tomato, garlic, salt, and pepper. Spread on toast and top with ham slices. Sprinkle generously with grated cheese.

Broil until cheese is melted and flecked with brown.

Yields 8 sandwiches.

Broiled Ham and Cheese Sandwich

2 tablespoons butter, softened
1/4 teaspoon thyme
    salt and pepper to taste
6 slices white bread
6 slices ham
6 thin slices Italian fontina cheese

Preheat broiler.

In a bowl, combine the butter, thyme, salt, and pepper. Toast bread on one side and spread untoasted sides with butter mixture. Place ham and fontina slices on buttered sides and arrange sandwiches on baking sheet.

Glaze under the broiler.

Yields 6 sandwiches.

Baked Ham, Gruyere, and Roquefort Sandwich

12 slices white toast, crusts removed
3 tablespoons butter, melted
12 thin slices Gruyere cheese
6 thin slices baked ham
1-1/2 cups grated Roquefort cheese
2 egg yolks
3 tablespoons dry white wine

Preheat oven to 400° F.

Brush one side of toast slices with butter. Place half the toasts on a work surface. Cut Gruyere and ham to fit toasts. Layer ham between two slices of cheese on each toast. Cover with remaining toast slices, buttered side down.

In a bowl, blend the Roquefort, egg yolks, and wine. Spread on top of each sandwich.

Bake 10 to 15 minutes until the topping is nicely browned.

Yields 6 sandwiches.

Broiled Bacon, Tomato, and Blue Cheese Sandwich

- 6 slices white bread
  butter
- 12 slices crisp bacon
- 18 thin slices tomato
- 6 tablespoons crumbled blue cheese

Preheat broiler.

Toast bread on one side and butter untoasted sides. Top buttered sides with bacon, tomato, and blue cheese. Broil until cheese melts.

Yields 6 sandwiches.

Curried Cabbage and Ham Sandwich

- 3 tablespoons mayonnaise
- 6 tablespoons minced chutney
- 1/2 teaspoon curry powder, or to taste
  salt to taste
- 1-1/2 cups shredded cabbage
- 12 slices rye bread
- 2 tablespoons butter
- 1 pound ham, sliced very thin
- 6 slices cheddar cheese
- 2 tablespoons butter

In a bowl, combine the mayonnaise, chutney, curry powder, and salt. Stir in the cabbage.

Butter the bread and top six slices with ham, cabbage mixture, and cheese slices. Place remaining bread slices on top, buttered side down.

Butter the outsides of sandwiches and cook on a griddle until browned on both sides.

Yields 6 sandwiches.

Saucisson en Croute

Sausage in French Bread

6 French bread rolls, or 1 loaf French bread

6 Italian sausages, cooked

Dijon mustard to taste

Preheat oven to 350°F.

Cut the ends off rolls, or cut loaf into sections as long as the sausages. With a wooden spoon handle or 1-inch-thick dowel, ream out rolls or bread.

Dip hot sausages into mustard and fill the rolls. Bake for about 5 minutes to heat the bread.

Yields 6 sandwiches.

Sauerkraut and Bratwurst Sandwich

1 quart sauerkraut, washed and drained

1 apple, peeled and thinly sliced

1 tablespoon caraway seeds, crushed

2 tablespoons vegetable oil

1 pound bratwurst

1 tablespoon butter

1/2 cup white wine

6 whole wheat pita loaves or 12 slices caraway rye bread

Dijon mustard to taste

In a medium-size skillet, saute the sauerkraut, apple, and caraway in oil for 3 minutes. Cover and simmer gently for 20 minutes.

In another skillet, saute the bratwurst in butter until browned on both sides. Pour off excess fat and add the wine. Cook until wine evaporates.

Stuff pita loaves with a generous quantity of sauerkraut and top with bratwurst. Serve mustard on the side.

If using caraway rye bread, arrange a layer of sauerkraut on half the slices. Split bratwurst lengthwise and arrange on sauerkraut. Cover with remaining bread slices.

Yields 6 sandwiches.

*2 Hot Sandwiches*

Sausage and Sauerkraut Sandwich

1-1/2 pounds pork sausage meat
   6 slices Gruyere cheese
   1 cup chopped sauerkraut
 1/8 teaspoon caraway seeds
    butter
   6 Kaiser or poppy seed rolls, split and toasted

Shape sausage meat into six patties. Saute in a skillet or broil. Top each with a cheese slice.

In a saucepan, heat the sauerkraut, caraway, and butter. Arrange roll bottoms on a plate and top with sauerkraut and sausage patties. Serve roll tops on the side.

Yields 6 sandwiches.

Fried Tomato and Bacon Sandwich

  6 1/2-inch thick slices tomato
    butter
  6 slices whole wheat or rye toast, buttered
12 slices crisp bacon

Saute tomatoes in butter until heated through and lightly browned. Arrange tomato slices on toast and top with bacon slices.

Yields 6 sandwiches.

Chapter 3
Vegetarian Sandwiches

Many restaurants will find vegetarian sandwiches a profitable addition to their menu. It is not only the diet-conscious who appreciate interesting combinations of food that are low in fat, high in complex carbohydrates, and lack animal protein. Many diners are interested in health and nutrition.

The recipes in this chapter are specifically designated as vegetarian, but other chapters contain recipes that are also suitable for the vegetarian.

Cheese Souffle Sandwich

- 3 eggs, separated
- 1/2 teaspoon salt
- 1/4 teaspoon dry mustard
- 1/8 teaspoon pepper
  cayenne pepper to taste
- 1 cup grated cheddar or chevre cheese
- 6 slices whole wheat bread, toasted

Preheat oven to 350° F.

In a bowl, beat the egg yolks, salt, mustard, pepper, and cayenne until light and lemon colored. Fold in the cheese.

Beat egg whites with a pinch of salt until stiff but not dry. Fold into the cheese mixture. Spread cheese mixture on toast and arrange on a baking sheet.

Bake for 10 to 12 minutes or until puffed and golden.

Yields 6 sandwiches.

Note: Any cheese that can be grated or crumbled may be substituted.

Particular attention should be paid to obtaining the freshest and most wholesome ingredients. Be firm with your suppliers to ensure that you never receive hard, green, flavorless tomatoes, old tough carrots, or rusty lettuces.

Cheese, Cucumber, and Radish Sandwich

3/4 cup peeled, minced, and seeded cucumber
1-1/2 cups minced radishes
    salt
12 slices Westphalian pumpernickel
6 ounces cream cheese

In a colander, combine cucumber and radishes and mix well. Sprinkle with salt and let drain 30 minutes. Rinse under cold running water, drain well, and toss in paper toweling.

Spread half the bread slices with cream cheese and top with a layer of cucumber mixture. Cover with remaining bread slices.

Yields 6 sandwiches.

Note: These can be served as open-faced sandwiches, if desired.

Green Pepper and Cheddar Cheese Sandwich

6 tablespoons butter

3 tablespoons sesame seeds

1 12-inch loaf Italian bread

1-1/3 cups grated cheddar cheese

1 green pepper, thinly sliced

Preheat oven to 400° F.

In a bowl, combine the butter and sesame seeds. Cut loaf in half lengthwise and spread each half with the butter mixture.

Arrange the bread on baking sheets, sprinkle generously with cheese, and arrange pepper slices on top. Bake for 10 minutes or until cheese melts. Cut into 6 sections and serve.

Yields 6 sandwiches.

Herbed Cheese Sandwich with Alfalfa Sprouts

8 ounces cream cheese

1/3 cup minced chives

5 teaspoons minced thyme

3/4 teaspoon salt

1/4 teaspoon pepper

8 thin slices pumpernickel bread

1 cup alfalfa sprouts

In a bowl, cream the cheese and beat in chives, thyme, salt, and pepper. Cover and chill for at least 1 hour.

Spread cheese mixture on bread and top with alfalfa sprouts. Serve as open-faced sandwiches.

Yields 8 sandwiches.

3 Vegetarian Sandwiches

Sandwiche a la Suisse

Gruyere and Olive Sandwich

12 large green olives, minced
 4 small gherkins, minced
 2 tablespoons mayonnaise
   butter
 6 thin slices whole wheat bread
 6 thin slices Gruyere cheese

Use a tea towel to squeeze the excess moisture from olives and gherkins. Bind with mayonnaise.

Butter bread slices and spread a layer of olive mixture on three slices. Place cheese on top and cover with remaining bread slices.

Yields 3 sandwiches.

Poppy Seed and Gruyere Sandwich

1/4 cup butter
1-1/2 tablespoons minced onion
   2 teaspoons poppy seeds
     cayenne pepper to taste
   6 slices white bread
1/2 cup grated Gruyere cheese

Preheat oven to 350° F.

In a bowl, combine the butter, onion, poppy seeds, and cayenne. Toast bread on one side and spread poppy seed butter on untoasted side. Sprinkle with cheese.

Bake about 10 minutes or until cheese melts.

Yields 6 sandwiches.

Cheddar and Walnut Sandwich

1/4 pound sharp cheddar cheese, grated

  8 tablespoons butter

    salt to taste

    paprika to taste

1/4 pound walnuts, thinly sliced

 12 slices whole wheat bread

Cream the cheese, butter, salt, and paprika together. Mix in nuts. Spread on half the bread slices and cover with remaining bread slices. Remove crusts if desired.

Yields 6 sandwiches.

Roquefort Cheese and Almond Sandwich

 9 ounces Roquefort cheese

 3 tablespoons butter

    Tabasco sauce to taste

12 slices whole wheat bread, very thinly sliced

 6 tablespoons minced salted almonds

In a bowl, combine the Roquefort, butter, and Tabasco and mix until soft and smooth.

Spread half the bread slices with cheese mixture and sprinkle with almonds. Cover with remaining bread slices.

Yields 6 sandwiches.

Vegetable Sandwich

1/2 cup minced cabbage
1/2 cup minced carrot
1/2 cup minced green pepper
1/2 cup minced celery
1/2 cup minced radishes
1/2 cup minced red onion
  6 slices white bread, toasted
  6 cups grated cheddar cheese
1/2 cup beer
    white pepper to taste
    cayenne pepper to taste
    dill pickles, optional

Preheat broiler.

In a bowl, combine the cabbage, carrot, green pepper, celery, radishes, and onion. Butter toast and spread each slice with 1/3 cup of vegetable mixture.

In a saucepan, melt the cheese in the beer and season with white pepper and cayenne.

Arrange sandwiches on heatproof serving dishes and coat with sauce. Broil until cheese is lightly browned. Garnish with pickles if desired.

Yields 6 sandwiches.

Avocado Sandwich

    butter
    salt and pepper to taste
12 slices white bread
 1 large avocado, peeled and seeded
    juice of 1 lemon

Season the butter with salt and pepper and spread on bread slices. Cut avocado into thin slices, toss with lemon juice, and marinate for 10 minutes.

Arrange avocado slices on half the bread slices. Cover with remaining bread slices.

Yields 6 sandwiches.

Carrot and Horseradish Sandwich

1 cup grated raw carrot
1 teaspoon grated horseradish
1 teaspoon Dijon mustard
1 tablespoon minced parsley
  mayonnaise
8 slices whole wheat bread, buttered
  butter

In a bowl, combine the carrots, horseradish, mustard, parsley, and just enough mayonnaise to bind. Mix well. Assemble sandwiches.

Yields 4 sandwiches.

Eggplant Sandwich

12 thin slices French bread
 6 eggplant slices, sauteed
 6 tomato slices, broiled
 6 onion rings, sauteed
 2 tablespoons grated Parmesan
   cheese

Preheat oven to 350° F.

Arrange six bread slices on a baking sheet and top with eggplant, tomato, onion, and grated cheese. Cover with remaining bread slices.

Bake for 10 minutes or until heated and cheese is slightly melted.

Yields 6 sandwiches.

Vegetarian Sandwiches

Toasted Mushroom Sandwich

8 tablespoons butter, melted
1 garlic clove, minced
1 tablespoon plus 1 teaspoon minced onion
1 pound mushrooms, minced
2 tablespoons heavy cream
1/4 teaspoon paprika
1/2 teaspoon salt
   pepper to taste
12 slices white bread

Preheat broiler.

Combine 2 tablespoons butter, garlic, and onion in a large skillet and saute until onion is golden. Add the mushrooms and cook for 3 minutes. Stir in the cream, paprika, salt, and pepper and cook, stirring, until most of the liquid has evaporated.

Spread on six slices of bread and top with remaining bread slices. Brush outsides of the sandwiches with remaining butter. Broil both sides until toasted.

Yields 6 sandwiches.

Bermuda Onion Sandwich

1 large Bermuda onion, thinly sliced
2 tablespoons salt
1 tablespoon sugar
2 tablespoons mayonnaise
6 slices white or whole wheat bread
3 tablespoons butter

In a bowl, combine the onion, salt, and sugar. Add enough ice water to cover. Let stand 1 hour. Drain well.

Combine onions and mayonnaise. Spread bread slices with butter and top with onion mixture.

Yields 6 sandwiches.

Tahini Sour Cream Sandwich with Sprouts

1/2 cup tahini
1/2 cup sour cream
3 tablespoons lemon juice
1 garlic clove, crushed
  salt to taste
6 slices pumpernickel bread
1-1/2 cups alfalfa sprouts

In a bowl, combine the tahini, sour cream, lemon juice, garlic, and salt. Let stand 1 hour.

Spread on bread slices and arrange sprouts on top. Serve as open-faced sandwiches.

Yields 6 sandwiches.

Pepper, Tomato, and Egg Sandwich

3 scallions, minced
3 green peppers, chopped
1/4 cup butter
3 tomatoes, peeled, seeded, and chopped
3 eggs, lightly beaten
  salt and pepper to taste
  summer savory to taste
6 pita loaves

In a skillet, saute the scallions and peppers in butter until soft but not brown. Add tomatoes and cook 3 minutes, or until most of the liquid has evaporated. Stir in the eggs, salt, pepper, and savory and cook, stirring, until eggs are just set.

Fill pita loaves. Serve hot or cold.

Yields 6 sandwiches.

3 Vegetarian Sandwiches

41

Tomato, Onion, and Basil Sandwich

3 large tomatoes, peeled, seeded, and sliced

salt

12 slices white bread

1/2 cup basil mayonnaise

1 Spanish onion, thinly sliced

Sprinkle tomato slices with salt and drain on a rack for 30 minutes.

Spread bread slices with mayonnaise. On six slices, layer onion, tomatoes, and more onion. Cover with remaining bread slices.

Yields 6 sandwiches.

Note: To make basil mayonnaise, fold 2 to 3 tablespoons minced fresh basil into 1/2 cup mayonnaise.

Tomato, Onion, and Coriander Sandwich

6 thin slices white bread

6 thin slices whole wheat bread

coriander butter (recipe follows)

5 plum tomatoes, thinly sliced

1 large Bermuda onion, thinly sliced

Spread bread slices with coriander butter and assemble sandwiches.

Yields 6 sandwiches.

Coriander Butter

3/4 cup butter

5 tablespoons minced coriander

1-1/2 teaspoons lemon juice

3/4 teaspoon ground coriander

salt and pepper to taste

In a bowl, cream the butter and beat in the coriander, lemon juice, ground coriander, and salt and pepper. Chill for at least 1 hour to develop flavor. Soften before spreading on bread.

Chapter 4

Submarines, Grinders, & Other Super Sandwiches

S uper sandwiches are composed of a multitude of compatible ingredients piled into whole loaves of bread (sometimes rolls for individual service) and often allowed to marinate and meld their flavors for at least 30 minutes before serving. Hot sandwiches of this type, however, must be served immediately after heating.

Their place of origin is probably around the Mediterranean, where the people of several countries enjoy similar sandwiches. The idea has certainly taken hold in the United States, where

Pain Jambon
Ham Sandwich

6 small French rolls, split
   butter
6 paper-thin slices baked ham

Butter both halves of the rolls. Place a thin slice of ham in each roll, wrap in foil, and weight heavily for at least 30 minutes. These sandwiches should be very flat.

Yields 6 sandwiches.

Note: These sandwiches are best if made with a bone-in ham, not a canned or reshaped ham.

we have submarines, grinders, heroes, poor boys, muffulettas, and others. The number and variety of fillings are countless. Some sandwich shops seem to believe that any Italian meal can be placed in a loaf of bread and served. You, however, will want to consider carefully the relationship of various ingredients. These recipes provide a wonderful sampling of the possibilities of such sandwiches, but use your imagination to develop new attractions for your menu.

Many of these sandwiches require weighting to compress the sandwich to a reasonable size and to concentrate the flavors. In the past, it was not uncommon to ride to a picnic seated on these sandwiches, which were wrapped in impeccably clean tea towels. Today we wrap them securely in foil, place them on a baking sheet, and cover them with another baking sheet. Cans of food or other weights are then placed on top. Let them stand for 30 minutes at room temperature or several hours in the refrigerator. If they must travel, wrap them in foil and put them at the bottom of a picnic basket or bag.

These sandwiches are served cut into sections or wedges, depending on the shape of the loaves. Although most of the sandwiches in this section call for white bread, you may substitute whole

Italian Sandwich

  1 loaf Italian bread, split horizontally
1/2 garlic clove
  1 cucumber, peeled, seeded, and thinly sliced
1/4 pound prosciutto, thinly sliced
  1 tomato, seeded and thinly sliced
  1 pimiento, sliced
  3 green olives, sliced
  6 anchovy fillets
    olive oil to taste
    vinegar to taste
    pepper to taste

Rub insides of the bread with the garlic clove and discard garlic. Arrange layers of cucumber, prosciutto, tomato, pimiento, olives, and anchovies on the bottom half. Sprinkle with olive oil, vinegar, and pepper to taste. Cover with the loaf top, weight the sandwich, and let stand for 30 minutes to 1-1/2 hours.

Yields 6 sandwiches.

wheat or rye. However, it is important that the crust be crisp and firm, or the juices may ooze out during the weighting period or the bread become so soggy that the sandwich falls apart. If you use pita loaves do not compress the filling and serve them immediately.

Pita Beef Sandwich

3 cups shredded lettuce
3 cups shredded raw spinach
1/2 cup minced scallion
   vinaigrette dressing to taste
6 pita loaves
12 tablespoons cream cheese
3/4 pound roast beef, thinly sliced
24 large Greek olives, pitted and sliced

In a bowl, combine the lettuce, spinach, scallion, and enough vinaigrette to coat lightly.

Cut the loaves in half and open each pocket. Spread the insides with cream cheese. Fill with the lettuce mixture and arrange beef slices and olives on top.

Yields 6 sandwiches.

Ratatouille and Sausage Pita Sandwich

      1 pound eggplant, peeled, 1-inch cubes

        salt and pepper to taste

      1 onion, minced

      1 green pepper, minced

      5 tablespoons olive oil

    1/2 pound Italian sausage, crumbled

      1 1-pound can Italian plum tomatoes

      3 garlic cloves, minced

      1 bay leaf

1-1/2 teaspoons minced basil

1-1/2 teaspoons minced thyme

      3 tablespoons minced parsley

      2 tablespoons grated Parmesan cheese

      6 pita loaves

Sprinkle the eggplant with salt and drain in a colander for 15 minutes.

In a skillet, saute onion and green pepper in 2 tablespoons olive oil for 3 minutes, stirring, until the onion is softened. Add the sausage, salt, and pepper and cook until the meat loses its color.

Transfer the ingredients to a bowl with a slotted spoon, leaving fat in the pan. Add 3 tablespoons of oil to the skillet and heat.

Pat eggplant dry with paper toweling and saute it, stirring, for 3 minutes. Add the sausage mixture, tomatoes, garlic, bay leaf, basil, and thyme. Cover and cook over low heat, stirring occasionally, for 30 minutes, or until thickened. Stir in the parsley and Parmesan. Discard the bay leaf. Cool. Use to fill pita loaves or, if desired, fill whole loaves of white or whole wheat bread.

Yields 6 sandwiches.

Tomato, Salami, and Mozzarella Sandwich

1 loaf Italian bread, split lengthwise

12 slices salami

butter

1/4 pound mushrooms, sliced

1/4 cup flour

1 cup medium cream

1/2 cup white wine

white pepper to taste

celery seed to taste

3 tomatoes, peeled and thinly sliced

4 to 6 slices mozzarella cheese

Preheat oven to 425° F.

Place bread, cut side up, on a baking sheet and bake until golden. Remove from oven. Arrange salami on the bread and set aside.

In a saucepan, melt 2 tablespoons butter and saute mushrooms until golden. Use a slotted spoon to scatter mushrooms over the salami.

Add enough butter to the pan to measure 1/4 cup. Stir in the flour and cook, stirring, for 3 minutes. Add cream and cook until thickened. Stir in the wine, pepper, and celery seed and cook until thickened and smooth.

Spread sauce over the mushrooms. Place overlapping tomato slices on top and cover with mozzarella slices. Bake until the cheese melts and the sandwich is heated.

Yields 6 sandwiches.

Submarines,
4 *Grinders,*
& Other Super Sandwiches

Muffuletta I

Olive, Salami, and Cheese Sandwich

1/2 cup pitted, oil-cured black olives, chopped

1/2 cup stuffed green olives, chopped

1/2 cup chopped mixed marinated vegetables

2/3 cup olive oil

1/4 cup minced parsley

  3 tablespoons lemon juice

  2 garlic cloves, minced

  1 teaspoon oregano

    pepper to taste

  1 10-inch round bread

1/4 pound salami, thinly sliced

1/4 pound provolone cheese, thinly sliced

1/4 pound prosciutto, thinly sliced

In a bowl, combine the olives, vegetables, oil, parsley, lemon juice, garlic, oregano, and pepper. Marinate overnight.

Split the loaf in half horizontally and remove the crumb, leaving shells 1/2-inch thick. Brush the insides with dressing from the vegetable salad.

Line the bottom of the loaf with salami slices. Spread on half the salad mixture and place provolone on top. Add remaining salad and layer prosciutto on top. Cover with top of loaf. Weight at least 30 minutes.

Yields 6 sandwiches.

Muffuletta II
Olive, Sausage, and Cheese Sandwich

1-1/2 cups stuffed olives, chopped

1-1/2 cups ripe olives, chopped

  2/3 cup olive oil

  1/3 cup minced parsley

    4 ounces pimientos, drained and chopped

    3 anchovy fillets, minced

    2 tablespoons capers

    1 tablespoon minced garlic

    1 tablespoon minced oregano

      pepper to taste

    1 9-inch round Italian bread

  1/4 pound Soppressato sausage, thinly sliced

  1/4 pound provolone cheese, thinly sliced

  1/4 pound mortadella sausage, thinly sliced

In a bowl, combine the olives, oil, parsley, pimientos, anchovies, capers, garlic, oregano, and pepper. Marinate overnight.

Drain the salad, reserving the dressing. Cut bread in half, horizontally, and remove the crumb, leaving 1/2-inch thick shells. Brush insides generously with reserved dressing.

Spoon half the salad into the bottom and press in firmly. Alternate layers of Soppressato, cheese, and mortadella in the shell, ending with a layer of mortadella. Mound remaining salad on top and cover with the loaf top. Wrap in foil, weight with 5 pounds, and chill for 30 minutes to 4 hours.

Yields 6 sandwiches.

Baked Sausage and Prosciutto Loaf

1 loaf French bread
1 leek, thinly sliced
2 tablespoons butter
1/4 pound Italian sausage, crumbled
1/4 pound spinach, wilted, drained, and chopped
1/4 pound prosciutto, thinly sliced
1/3 cup minced parsley
1 large egg, lightly beaten
1-1/2 teaspoons minced sage
    nutmeg to taste
    salt and pepper to taste
1/4 pound Gruyere cheese, grated
3 tablespoons butter, melted
1 egg, lightly beaten

Preheat oven to 200° F.

Cuff off top third of the bread and remove crumb from both sections, leaving shells 1/2-inch thick. Dry shells in the oven for 20 minutes.

Raise oven temperature to 350° F. Spread the crumb on a baking sheet and oven dry for 10 minutes, or until lightly golden. Pulverize the crumb in a blender or processor.

In a skillet, saute the leek in butter until soft. Transfer to a bowl. Saute the sausage until it is no longer pink. Drain off excess fat and add the sausage to the bowl.

Squeeze the spinach dry and add to the bowl. Chop the prosciutto and add to the bowl with parsley, one egg, sage, nutmeg, salt, pepper, and cheese. Mix well.

Brush insides of the shells with melted butter. Mound sausage mixture inside the shell. Brush cut edges of the loaf with remaining egg and fit loaf together.

Wrap in foil and bake in preheated 350° F. oven for 30 minutes. Cool to room temperature and cut into six sections.

Yields 6 sandwiches.

Prosciutto and Cheese Sandwich

1 loaf Italian bread, split horizontally

6 to 8 slices Port du Salut or Italian fontina cheese

1/4 cup minced leek

12 slices prosciutto or pastrami

1 tablespoon capers

2 large eggs, separated

1 cup mayonnaise

Preheat oven to 425°F.

Place bottom half of the bread on a baking sheet and bake until golden. (Use top half for another recipe or double the ingredients.)

Arrange cheese on the bread and sprinkle with leeks. Place prosciutto and capers on top.

Beat egg yolks and fold into the mayonnaise. Beat egg whites until stiff but not dry. Fold into the mayonnaise and spread over the sandwich.

Bake for 8 to 10 minutes or until the topping is golden.

Yields 3 to 6 sandwiches.

Greek Country Salad Loaf

1 sesame-seeded, doughnut-shaped loaf

butter

1 cucumber, peeled and sliced

2 tomatoes, seeded and chopped

6 ounces feta cheese, crumbled

5 ounces salami, julienne

24 pitted ripe Greek olives

1 avocado, peeled and sliced

3 tablespoons capers

8 anchovy fillets

4 tablespoons olive oil

2 tablespoons lemon juice

1/2 teaspoon oregano

salt and pepper to taste

Slice bread in half horizontally and remove crumb, leaving 1/2-inch thick shells. Butter shells generously.

Place cucumber, tomato, cheese, salami, olives, avocado, capers, and anchovies in a bowl. Mix oil, lemon juice, oregano, salt, and pepper in another bowl. Pour over salad ingredients and toss gently but completely.

Spoon into bottom shell and cover with top shell. Weight for 30 minutes.

Yields 6 sandwiches.

Submarines, Grinders, & Other Super Sandwiches

4

51

Pan Bagna I

1 1-pound loaf French bread, split horizontally
1/2 cup water
1/2 teaspoon salt
1/2 to 1 cup olive oil
2 tomatoes, sliced
4 artichoke hearts, cooked and sliced
1/4 cup sliced mushrooms
1 celery heart, cut in strips
1/4 pound black olives
8 to 10 anchovy fillets

Place bread halves on a work surface. Combine water and salt and stir until salt is dissolved. Brush or sprinkle bread halves with the salt mixture. Sprinkle with oil to taste.

When bread is well impregnated, but not soaked, place tomatoes, artichoke hearts, mushrooms, celery, olives, and anchovies on bottom half. Cover with top half and weight for at least 30 minutes.

Yields 6 sandwiches.

Pan Bagna II

1 loaf French bread, split horizontally
olive oil to taste
1 red onion, thinly sliced
1 green pepper, thinly sliced
1 tomato, thinly sliced
8 anchovy fillets
1 cup tuna fish, drained and flaked
1/2 cup pitted ripe olives, sliced
salt and pepper to taste
1 garlic clove, split

Brush insides of the loaf with olive oil and let it soak in for a few minutes. On the bottom half, place the onion, green pepper, tomato, anchovies, tuna, and olives. Season with salt and pepper.

Brush top half of the loaf with the garlic clove, pressing to extract garlic juices. Discard garlic. Press the top half onto the sandwich and weight for 2 hours.

Yields 6 sandwiches.

Pan Bagna III

 1 tablespoon red wine vinegar
1/4 teaspoon Dijon mustard
   salt and pepper to taste
1/4 cup olive oil
 1 loaf French bread, split
   horizontally
1/2 garlic clove
 2 tomatoes, thinly sliced
 1 tablespoon minced scallion
 4 anchovy fillets
12 black olives, sliced
2/3 cup cooked green beans
1/2 cup slivered green pepper
1/2 cup sliced mushrooms
 2 tablespoons minced parsley

In a bowl, combine the vinegar, mustard, salt, pepper, and oil and mix well.

Rub cut sides of the bread with the garlic clove. Discard garlic. Drizzle half the dressing over the bottom half of the loaf.

Layer tomatoes, scallions, anchovies, olives, beans, green pepper, and mushrooms over the dressing and sprinkle with parsley, salt, and pepper. Drizzle remaining dressing on the top half of loaf and cover the sandwich. Weight for at least 1 hour.

Yields 6 sandwiches.

La Mediatrice I

 1 12-inch loaf French bread, split
   horizontally
   butter, melted
36 mussels, scrubbed and bearded
 1 egg, lightly beaten
   oil for deep frying
   guacamole (see following recipe)

Preheat oven to 425° F.

Remove the crumb from loaf halves, leaving 1/2-inch thick shells. In a processor, pulverize the crumb and set aside. Brush shells with butter and bake until golden.

In 1 inch of water, steam the mussels until they open. Remove mussels from shells. Dip mussels into the egg and then into reserved bread crumbs. Deep fry at 370° F. until golden. Drain on paper toweling.

Fill bottom loaf half with guacamole and top with mussels. Cover with the top loaf half.

Yields 6 sandwiches.

Note: Add shredded lettuce and chopped tomato to the sandwich if desired.

Submarines,
4 Grinders,
& Other Super
Sandwiches

Guacamole

　　1　ripe avocado, peeled and
　　　　chopped
　　1　tomato, peeled, seeded, and
　　　　chopped
1-1/2　teaspoons minced onion
1-1/2　teaspoons white wine vinegar
　1/2　teaspoon lime juice
　1/2　teaspoon chili powder
　1/4　teaspoon minced garlic
　　　　salt and pepper to taste

Prepare 1 hour before using.

Place avocado, tomato, and onion in a
processor with the vinegar, lime
juice, chili powder, garlic, and salt
and pepper. Chop coarsely with
on-off turns.

Yields about 1-1/2 cups.

La Mediatrice II

　　　6　French rolls
　　　　　butter
18 to 24　oysters
　　　　　salt and pepper to taste
　　　　　Tabasco sauce to taste
　　　　　cream, optional

Preheat oven to 425° F.

Cut off tops of the rolls and scoop out
the crumb. Brush insides with butter
and bake on a baking sheet until
golden.

Saute the oysters in butter until
plump and the edges begin to curl.
Season with salt, pepper, and
Tabasco. Place the oysters in the
rolls, sprinkle with a little hot cream,
if desired, and cover with roll tops.
Serve hot.

Yields 6 sandwiches.

Sandwich Torte

1 large, round loaf white bread
1/2 cup chopped almonds
3/4 cup chopped stuffed olives
    mayonnaise
1 cup minced cooked shrimp
1/2 cup butter, softened
4 teaspoons tomato paste
    cayenne pepper to taste
    salt to taste
5 hard-cooked eggs, minced
1/2 cup butter, softened
1-1/2 teaspoons curry powder
1 cucumber, thinly sliced
    cherry tomatoes for garnish
    lettuce leaves for garnish

With a bread knife, remove the top, sides, and bottom of the loaf, keeping the shape round. Cut the bread horizontally into four equal slices. (They should look like thin layers of cake.)

In a bowl, combine the almonds, olives, and enough mayonnaise to bind. Spread on one slice of bread and cover with a second slice.

Combine the shrimp, 1/2 cup butter, tomato paste, cayenne, and salt and spread on the second bread slice. Cover with a third slice.

Combine the eggs, remaining butter, curry powder, salt, and pepper and spread on the third bread slice. Cover with the fourth slice and press the loaf together gently to form a cake.

Wrap in dampened paper toweling and cover with plastic wrap. Chill until fillings are firm.

Shortly before serving, transfer loaf to a serving platter and spread the whole loaf with a thin layer of mayonnaise. Score the top of the loaf into wedges. Use cucumber, tomatoes, and lettuce to garnish the loaf. Thin slices of cucumbers can be wrapped like a cornucopia around a cherry tomato and arranged in the center and around the outer edges. Place lettuce around the base. Or, cut thin sections of cucumber, form twists on each wedge, and arrange slices of cherry tomato on the cucumber.

Yields 6 to 8 wedges.

Pain Basquaise

4 tablespoons olive oil

4 red peppers, peeled and julienned

2/3 cup tuna packed in olive oil

salt and pepper to taste

2 tablespoons red wine vinegar

4 tablespoons minced parsley

3 garlic cloves, minced

2 loaves French bread, halved lengthwise

4 hard-cooked eggs, sliced

In a skillet, heat 3 tablespoons oil and cook peppers until hot. Add the tuna, salt, and pepper and cook, stirring, until tuna is flaked and heated. Add the vinegar, 2 tablespoons parsley, and garlic. Cook until vinegar has evaporated. Remove from heat and season with salt and pepper.

Place bread on a baking sheet and toast until warm and crisp, but not brown. Top two halves with tuna mixture and garnish with eggs. Drizzle a little oil on top, sprinkle with remaining parsley, and cover with bread tops.

Yields 6 sandwiches.

Rump Steak Sandwich

1 2-pound rump steak

salt and pepper to taste

rosemary or garlic butter

1 loaf French bread, split horizontally

Preheat broiler.

Broil steak to desired degree and let rest at least 5 minutes. Season with salt and pepper.

Toast both bread halves and butter them. Slice the steak thinly and arrange on bottom bread half. Cover with the top.

Yields 4 to 6 sandwiches.

Note: For variety use horseradish butter and garnish with tomato slices.

Peacemaker, Poor Boy, or Oyster Loaf

1 pint medium-size shucked oysters

1/4 teaspoon cayenne pepper

    black pepper to taste

2 eggs

1/2 cup evaporated milk

    pinch of salt

1 cup unsifted cornstarch

1-1/2 cups soft bread crumbs

1 loaf French bread

4 tablespoons butter, melted

    oil for deep frying

1/2 cup Creole Tartar sauce (see following recipe)

1-1/2 cups shredded lettuce

1 tomato, 1/4-inch thick slices

Preheat oven to 375° F.

Pat oysters dry on paper towels and season with red and black pepper. In a bowl, beat eggs with milk and salt. Spread cornstarch on a piece of waxed paper and bread crumbs on another piece.

Roll oysters in cornstarch, dip in eggs, and roll in crumbs. Arrange in one layer on a plate and chill.

Slice bread in half horizontally and remove crumb from both sections. Brush with melted butter and bake for 15 minutes, or until crisp and lightly browned.

Heat oil to 375° F. Deep fry oysters until golden. Drain on paper towels.

Spread Creole sauce on the bread halves. Scatter lettuce on the bottom half and arrange tomato slices on top. Cover with oysters and add loaf top.

Yields 6 sandwiches.

Note: Instead of tomatoes and Creole Tartar sauce, you can spread the loaf with a mixture of 1/2 cup chili sauce, 2 tablespoons horseradish, 2 teaspoons lemon juice, and 1/4 teaspoon Worcestershire sauce.

Submarines, 4 Grinders, & Other Super Sandwiches

Creole Tartar Sauce

3 egg yolks
1 tablespoon Creole mustard
1/4 teaspoon cayenne pepper
1-1/2 teaspoons salt
1-1/2 cups olive oil
1/2 cup minced scallions
1/2 cup minced parsley
1/2 cup minced dill pickles

In a processor, combine the egg yolks, mustard, cayenne, and salt. With the machine running, pour in the oil in a slow steady stream. Fold in scallions, parsley, and pickles.

Yields about 2 cups.

Bookmaker Sandwich

1 loaf French bread, split horizontally
butter
2 1/2-inch thick sirloin steaks
salt and pepper to taste
horseradish to taste
dry mustard to taste

Spread both bread halves generously with butter. Broil the steaks until rare. Season with salt and pepper and sprinkle both sides with horseradish and mustard.

Assemble sandwich and weight with at least 5 pounds for 30 minutes or more. Unwrap and cut into sections.

Yields 6 sandwiches.

Beef, Potato, and Tomato Loaf

    6 ounces marinated mush-
      rooms, thinly sliced
    2 tablespoons tarragon vinegar
  1/2 teaspoon Dijon mustard
    1 garlic clove, minced
      salt and pepper to taste
    2 shallots, minced
  1/4 cup minced parsley
    1 pound small potatoes, boiled
      and sliced
    2 cups cherry tomatoes, halved
1-1/4 pounds rare roast beef or
      steak, cut in strips
      butter
    1 10-inch round crusty loaf
      bread

Drain mushroom juices into a bowl
and stir in vinegar, mustard, garlic,
salt, pepper, shallots, and parsley.

Add mushrooms to dressing with
potatoes, tomatoes, and beef. Mix
well.

Slice loaf in half horizontally and
remove crumb, leaving 1/2-inch thick
shells. Butter bread generously. Fill
bottom half with meat and potato
mixture and cover with top, pressing
down. Weight for at least 30 minutes.
Cut into wedges.

Yields 6 sandwiches.

Veal and Pepper Submarine Sandwich

1-1/2 pounds veal cutlets, in 1-inch squares
1-1/2 teaspoons salt
    pepper to taste
1/2 cup flour
  8 tablespoons olive oil
  1 cup minced onions
  1 teaspoon minced garlic
1/2 cup dry white wine
  2 red peppers, peeled
  2 green peppers, peeled
  1 loaf Italian bread, split horizontally

Sprinkle veal with salt and pepper. Dredge in flour, shaking off the excess.

Heat 4 tablespoons oil in a skillet. Saute veal in batches until golden and set aside. Add more oil as needed. Pour off all but 3 tablespoons of oil. Saute the onion and garlic until soft and lightly colored. Pour in the wine and return veal to pan. Cut peppers into 1-inch squares and add to pan. Simmer, covered, for 5 minutes. Correct seasoning with salt and pepper.

Fill bottom half of the loaf with veal and peppers and cover with the top.

Yields 2 to 4 sandwiches.

Syrian Sandwich

4 tomatoes, peeled, seeded, and chopped
2-1/2 tablespoons olive oil
1/4 cup pine nuts
2 teaspoons olive oil
1 cup chopped onions
1-1/2 pounds lamb, ground
1/4 cup minced parsley
1/4 cup chopped green pepper
1 tablespoon lemon juice
1 tablespoon vinegar
1-1/2 teaspoons salt
1/4 teaspoon cayenne pepper
1/4 teaspoon allspice
6 pita loaves

In a saucepan, cook the tomatoes in 1-1/2 tablespoons oil, covered, for 5 minutes. Uncover and cook, stirring occasionally, for 15 minutes or until a thick puree.

In a skillet, saute pine nuts in 2 teaspoons olive oil. Drain on paper towels. Add 1 tablespoon olive oil to the skillet and saute onions until lightly browned. Add the lamb and cook until it loses its color. Add the parsley, green pepper, lemon juice, vinegar, salt, cayenne, and allspice. Cook, stirring, for 3 minutes. Add tomato puree and cook, stirring, for 2 minutes. Add pine nuts. Cool to warm and fill pita loaves.

Yields 6 sandwiches.

Submarines, 4 Grinders, & Other Super Sandwiches

Chapter 5
Club Sandwiches

Club sandwiches are so popular that they are sold in almost every establishment, from the local diner to the four-star restaurant. They appeal to men, women, and children alike. In addition, they are easy to prepare and their ingredients are basic to most kitchens.

The perfect club sandwich begins with a slice of crisp, dry toast, spread lightly with butter and mayonnaise and topped with neatly arranged lettuce leaves and thin slices of chicken. Another slice of buttered toast, spread with mayonnaise, is added and topped with lettuce, thinly sliced

Caviar and Tomato Club Sandwich

  3 slices buttered toast
    mayonnaise to taste
1/4 cup caviar
  1 slice Bermuda onion
  2 slices tomato
    watercress sprigs

Place a toast slice on a plate and spread with mayonnaise and caviar. Place onion on top and then another slice of toast spread with mayonnaise. Arrange tomato slices and watercress on top and add the last toast slice.

Yields 1 sandwich.

Note: You may use red or black caviar, or lumpfish, white fish, or salmon caviar. Imported Russian or Iranian caviar is not recommended. Such prized items should be served on their own. Pressed caviar is also acceptable.

tomato, and crisp bacon slices. A final slice of toast, spread with butter and mayonnaise, completes the sandwich. Club sandwiches are usually cut into four triangles and arranged with one point of each triangle pointing upward. Each section is held together with wooden skewers. If the sandwiches are made with breads that will not hold up to this presentation, consider the comfort of the diner and cut the sandwiches into servings that are easy to manage. Also, when using pumpernickel and rye breads that often must be sliced thicker than white, two slices of bread may prove more desirable than three. In fact there may be some precedent for using only two slices of bread. James Beard has written that he recalls the sandwich originally being made with two slices and not the currently popular three.

Although white bread is customary for a club sandwich, the choice of bread is up to the chef or the customer. A choice of breads can increase profits by providing variety for the bored customer. Try these sandwiches on rye, whole wheat, or French bread, or even on Kaiser or poppy seed rolls. If you have an in-house baker who can prepare herbed sandwich breads, so much the better. Whatever bread you use should be toasted, with the possible exception of the rolls.

Crabmeat Club Sandwich

 3 slices buttered toast
   mayonnaise to taste
1/2 cup flaked crabmeat
 2 thin slices tomato
1/2 cup minced hard-cooked egg
 1 teaspoon minced celery
   watercress sprigs

Spread the toast with mayonnaise. Add just enough mayonnaise to bind the crabmeat and spread on one toast slice. Cover with tomato slices and another toast slice.

In a small bowl, combine the egg and celery with just enough mayonnaise to bind. Spread on the toast and garnish with watercress sprigs. Cover with remaining toast.

Yields 1 sandwich.

Oyster Club Sandwich

2 slices white toast

   lettuce leaves

4 large oysters, fried (see Peacemaker Sandwich)

   horseradish to taste

1 slice whole wheat toast

3 slices white chicken meat

4 slices crisp bacon

2 slices tomato

1 tablespoon tartar sauce

Cover one slice of toast with a lettuce leaf. Arrange oysters on top and spread lightly with horseradish.

Add the whole wheat toast and top with chicken, bacon, and tomato slices. Garnish with tartar sauce and a lettuce leaf. Cover with remaining white toast.

Yields 1 sandwich.

Salmon Club Sandwich

3 slices buttered toast

   mayonnaise to taste

   lettuce leaves

1/2 cup warm poached salmon, flaked

1 large slice tomato, broiled

2 to 3 slices crisp bacon

Spread the toast with mayonnaise. Arrange a lettuce leaf on one slice and cover with salmon. Add another slice of toast and top with tomato and bacon slices and a lettuce leaf. Cover with remaining toast.

Yields 1 sandwich.

Chicken Club Sandwich (The Original)

3 slices buttered toast
  mayonnaise to taste
  lettuce leaves
3 thin slices white chicken meat
2 slices crisp bacon
2 thin slices tomato

Spread toast slices with mayonnaise. Arrange a lettuce leaf on one slice. Cover with chicken slices and another slice of toast. Add a lettuce leaf and bacon and tomato slices. Cover with remaining toast.

Yields 1 sandwich.

Super French Club Sandwich

1 loaf French bread
  butter
  shredded lettuce
1/2 pound white chicken meat, thinly sliced
2 tomatoes, thinly sliced
6 slices crisp bacon
  mayonnaise to taste

Cut French bread in half horizontally and butter thoroughly. Arrange a layer of lettuce on the bottom half and place chicken, tomato, and bacon slices on top. Brush the inside of the top half with mayonnaise and cover the sandwich. To serve, cut into 2-inch-wide sections.

Yields 4 servings.

Queen Club Sandwich

3 slices buttered toast
  lettuce leaves
1/2 cup minced chicken
  mayonnaise to taste
1/4 cup mushrooms, sauteed

Arrange a lettuce leaf on a toast slice. Combine chicken and enough mayonnaise to bind and add to lettuce. Cover with toast slice. Arrange mushrooms on the toast and top with remaining toast.

Yields 1 sandwich.

Bacon, Chicken, and Anchovy Club Sandwich

3 slices buttered toast
  mayonnaise to taste
  lettuce
2 slices crisp bacon
3 slices white chicken meat
3 or 4 anchovy fillets
2 thin slices tomato

Spread the toast with mayonnaise. Cover one slice of toast with lettuce and bacon and top with another slice. Arrange chicken, anchovies, and tomato on top and cover with remaining toast.

Yields 1 sandwich.

5 *Club Sandwiches*

Liver, Corned Beef, and Salami Club Sandwich

2 chicken livers
butter
1/4 teaspoon minced onion
Dijon mustard to taste
salt to taste
3 slices rye toast
2 ounces corned beef, thinly sliced
lettuce leaves
1-1/2 ounces salami, thinly sliced

In a small skillet, saute the chicken livers in butter until browned outside but pink inside. In a processor, puree the livers with the onion and mustard. Correct seasoning with salt.

Spread toast with a little mustard. Arrange corned beef on one slice and cover with a lettuce leaf and a second slice of toast. Spread the second slice with the chicken liver mixture and top with lettuce and salami. Place remaining toast on top.

Yields 1 sandwich.

Bacon, Chicken Liver, and Tomato Club Sandwich

3 slices buttered toast
mayonnaise to taste
lettuce leaves
2 slices crisp bacon
2 chicken livers, broiled medium rare
1 large slice tomato
watercress sprigs

Spread toast with mayonnaise. Cover one slice with lettuce and bacon. Add another slice of toast and cover with sliced chicken livers, tomato, and watercress sprigs. Cover with remaining toast.

Yields 1 sandwich.

Chapter 6

Tea Sandwiches

In recent years, many hotels and some restaurants have reinstituted a mid- to late-afternoon tea hour. Harried shoppers, sightseers, and office workers seem to appreciate a light snack at that time of day. You will appreciate the additional profits generated by using your lobby or dining room during otherwise empty hours.

Tea sandwiches must be the most delicate and fragile of all sandwiches. The bread should be cut paper-thin. To do this by hand, cut off the crust from one side of an unsliced loaf of bread. Butter this side and cut off a thin slice with a long, very

Dried Fruit and Nut Tea Sandwich

1/2 cup dried figs

1/2 cup raisins

1/2 cup blanched peanuts, walnuts, or almonds

1 tablespoon orange marmalade

20 thin slices white bread

1 cup cream cheese

In a processor, grind the figs, raisins, and nuts to a relatively smooth mixture. Blend in the marmalade.

Spread bread slices with the cream cheese and then with the fruit mixture.

Yields 40 sandwiches.

thin, sharp knife. Butter again and cut another slice. Of course, the easiest method is to use an electric slicing machine and butter the bread after it is sliced. The butter must be soft, however, or it will tear the bread. Although firm, even-textured white bread can be sliced very thinly, such breads as rye and whole wheat often have to be sliced thicker to prevent crumbling.

The fillings should be flavorful and delicate. If you plan to use the same filling on different types of breads, it may be necessary to taste a sample of each to determine if the flavor of the filling is evident, or if it is overwhelmed by the flavor of the bread.

Any soft sandwich filling can be used to make pinwheel sandwiches. These are made by spreading the filling on long slices of bread and rolling up from the short side. The sandwich must be wrapped securely in plastic wrap and chilled for an hour before serving. Each roll is then cut into 1/4-inch-thick pinwheels. You can also make cigarettes by using a standard 4-by-4-inch slice of bread and rolling it tightly into a thin tube. Again, it must be wrapped and chilled to set the shape.

Canton Ginger Sandwich

   3 ounces cream cheese, softened
1 to 2 tablespoons heavy cream
   2 tablespoons minced ginger in syrup
 1/2 cup minced blanched almonds
   1 teaspoon lemon juice
     salt to taste
 1/4 teaspoon paprika
4 to 8 slices white toast

In a processor, cream the cheese and heavy cream until smooth. Add the ginger, almonds, lemon juice, salt, and paprika with on–off turns. If the mixture is too thin, chill to firm.

Spread on the toast. Serve open-faced or put two slices together.

Yields 16 to 32 sandwiches.

Smoked Salmon and
Caviar Sandwich
(See page 2.)

Shrimp and Pork
Steamed Buns
(See page 116.)

Chicken, Ham, and
Walnut Tea
Sandwich, Pimiento
Cheese Ribbon
Sandwich, Canton
Ginger Sandwich
(See pages 79, 70, and 72.)

Bacon, Chicken Liver, and Tomato Club Sandwich
(See page 68.)

Calzone
(See page 110.)

Chicken Club Sandwich
(See page 66.)

Avocado and Bacon
Sandwich
(See page 12.)

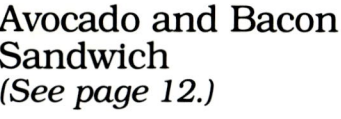

Ham, Egg, and Pepper
Croque-Monsieur
(See page 107.)

All tea sandwiches should have the crusts removed, unless they are made on finger rolls. After removing the crusts, cut the finished sandwich into small triangles, squares, or fingers. Or use round or other shaped cutters to cut decorative sandwiches. For a special effect, cut out the center of the top slice of the sandwich and insert an identical-size cutout from a different type of bread. Or leave the filling exposed.

Tea sandwich fillings may be served in small cocktail puffs or finger rolls, if desired. Whatever types or shapes of bread you use, try to have the bread flavors or shapes mirror the different fillings. For example, serve turkey on white squares, ham on white fingers, smoked oysters in puffs, and shrimp in finger rolls.

When preparing your own fillings or estimating the number of sandwiches needed, use the following as a guide. The average 4-by-4 slice of bread requires about 2-1/2 teaspoons of creamed butter and about 1-1/2 tablespoons of ground or chopped filling. Therefore, 1 cup of creamed butter and about 1 cup of filling are required for 20 slices of bread (or 10 full-size sandwiches). This yields about 40 tea sandwiches, enough to serve 7 or 8 guests. If you are going to offer a tea menu, you will want to include cookies and cakes in addition to the sandwiches.

Walnut Orange Cheese Sandwich

     1 cup cream cheese
 1/2 cup heavy cream
 1/2 cup walnuts
       salt to taste
       paprika to taste
    20 thin slices white bread, buttered
     6 ounces orange marmalade
       Dijon mustard to taste

In a bowl, combine the cheese, cream, walnuts, salt, and paprika. Mix well.

Spread 10 slices of bread with the cheese mixture. Combine the marmalade and mustard. Spread over the cheese mixture and cover with remaining bread slices.

Yields 40 sandwiches.

Pimiento Cheese Ribbon Sandwich

1/2 pound cheddar cheese, grated

1/2 cup drained, minced pimiento

2 tablespoons mayonnaise

1 tablespoon vinegar

1/4 teaspoon sugar

16 very thin slices whole wheat bread

In a processor, combine the cheese, pimiento, mayonnaise, vinegar, and sugar. Mix until combined but with bits of pimiento still showing.

Spread 12 slices of bread with the cheese mixture. Make four stacks of three slices each and put remaining bread slices on top of each stack. Cover and chill for at least 1 hour.

Cut off crusts and cut each stack into 1/4-inch-thick slices to make ribbon sandwiches.

Yields about 48 sandwiches.

Camembert and Radish Pinwheel Sandwich

1 loaf fine white bread, unsliced

1 cup butter

2 cups Camembert cheese, mashed

1/2 cup minced radish

With a sharp knife, remove crusts from the bread. Butter one long side of the bread.

In a bowl, combine the Camembert and radish and mix well. Spread on top of the butter and with a thin sharp knife cut off a slice of bread. Roll the bread from the short side into a roll. Wrap in plastic wrap and chill for at least 1 hour.

Repeat procedure with remaining ingredients. To serve cut into 1/4-inch-thick slices.

Yields about 64 sandwiches.

Rolled Watercress Tea Sandwich

12 thin slices white bread
3/4 cup butter, softened
1 bunch watercress sprigs

Trim crusts from the bread and spread with butter. Arrange watercress sprigs along one side of the bread letting a few leaves extend over the edges. Roll the bread into tubes. Wrap in plastic wrap and chill for at least 1 hour.

Yields 12 sandwiches.

Watercress Pinwheel Sandwich

1 loaf fine-textured white bread, unsliced
1 cup butter
3 cups minced watercress
2 teaspoons lemon juice
salt to taste
mayonnaise

Slice the bread lengthwise into thin slices and spread with butter. (If doing this by hand, it is easier to spread the bread with butter and then slice.)

In a bowl, combine the watercress, lemon juice, salt, and just enough mayonnaise to bind. Spread on a bread slice and roll up from the short side. Wrap in plastic wrap and chill for at least 1 hour. Cut into 1/4-inch-thick slices.

Yields about 64 sandwiches.

6 **Tea Sandwiches**

Spiced Cucumber Sandwich

2 cucumbers, thinly sliced
3 garlic cloves, split
1 tablespoon soy sauce
1/2 teaspoon salt
    Tabasco sauce to taste
    vinegar
24 slices white bread
    mayonnaise

Place cucumbers in a 1-quart container. Add the garlic, soy sauce, salt, Tabasco, and just enough vinegar to cover. Chill for 12 hours. Drain cucumbers, saving the vinegar to use again.

Spread bread slices with mayonnaise and cover half the slices with cucumbers. Cover with remaining bread and cut into shapes, removing the crusts.

Yields 48 sandwiches.

Dilled Salmon and Cucumber Sandwich

6 ounces smoked salmon
1/4 cup sour cream
1-1/2 teaspoons lemon juice
2 teaspoons minced dill
    salt and pepper to taste
12 thin slices white bread
1 seedless cucumber, thinly sliced
    sprigs of dill

In a processor, puree the salmon, sour cream, lemon juice, dill, salt, and pepper. Spread half the bread slices with the salmon mixture. Arrange cucumber slices on top and cover with remaining bread.

Remove the crusts, cut into shapes, and garnish the top of each sandwich with dill.

Yields about 24 sandwiches.

Chive Sandwich

10 slices white bread
1/2 cup anchovy butter
4 hard-cooked eggs, sieved
3 tablespoons minced chives
2 tablespoons mayonnaise
   sprigs of parsley

Spread bread slices with anchovy butter.

In a bowl, combine the eggs, chives, and enough mayonnaise to bind. Assemble sandwiches, cut into shapes, and garnish each sandwich with parsley sprigs.

Yields about 20 sandwiches.

Curried Egg and Smoked Oyster Sandwich

8 large smoked oysters, minced
3 hard-cooked eggs, minced
1 teaspoon curry powder
1/2 teaspoon grated onion
   mayonnaise
   salt and pepper to taste
8 thin slices bread, buttered

In a bowl, combine the oysters, eggs, curry powder, onion, and just enough mayonnaise to bind. Season with salt and pepper.

Assemble four sandwiches and cut into smaller shapes.

Yields about 16 sandwiches.

Note: This filling is suitable for cocktail puffs.

Smoked Oyster Tea Sandwich

1 3-1/2-ounce can smoked oysters
1/2 cup mayonnaise
   horseradish to taste
   lemon juice to taste
   butter
6 finger rolls
   minced parsley

Drain oysters of their oil.

Combine with mayonnaise, horseradish, and lemon juice and mix well.

Split the rolls almost, but not completely, in half and butter the insides. Fill the rolls. Sprinkle with parsley.

Yields 6 sandwiches.

6 Tea Sandwiches

Sardine and Celery Sandwich

1 can boneless sardines, drained
  Dijon mustard to taste
  lemon juice to taste
3 tablespoons minced celery
8 thin slices bread, buttered

In a bowl, mash the sardines and stir in mustard and lemon juice. Mix in the celery. Spread the mixture on half the bread slices. Assemble sandwiches and cut into shapes.

Yields 16 sandwiches.

Shrimp Sandwich

6 finger rolls
1/2 cup mayonnaise
1-1/2 teaspoons cognac
1 cup small shrimp, cooked, peeled, and deveined

Split the rolls lengthwise and spread with mayonnaise mixed with cognac. Line the shrimp along the bottom of the roll and cover with the top.

Yields 6 sandwiches.

Roast Beef and Horseradish Tea Sandwich

20 thin slices white bread
 1 cup horseradish butter
10 slices roast beef
  salt to taste

Spread bread slices with horseradish butter. Arrange roast beef on half the slices and season with salt. Cover with remaining slices and cut into sections.

Yields 40 sandwiches.

Ham and Chutney Tea Sandwich

20 thin slices white bread
1 cup mustard butter
1-1/2 cups minced chutney
10 thin slices baked ham

Spread bread slices with mustard butter. Spread half the slices with chutney. Arrange ham slices on chutney and cover with remaining bread slices.

Yields about 40 sandwiches.

Smoked Turkey and Curry Sandwich

20 thin slices whole wheat bread
1 cup curry butter
20 thin slices smoked turkey
3/4 cup ginger marmalade

Spread bread slices with curry butter. Arrange turkey on half the slices. Spread remaining bread with ginger marmalade and place on top of turkey.

Yields 40 sandwiches.

6 Tea Sandwiches

Chicken and Watercress Sandwich

20 slices white bread
 1 cup curry butter
3/4 cup mayonnaise
 2 bunches watercress sprigs
20 thin slices cooked chicken
     breast

Spread bread slices with curry butter and then with mayonnaise. Arrange half the watercress on 10 bread slices. Top with chicken and the remainder of the watercress. Place remaining bread on top.

Yields about 40 sandwiches.

Turkey Tea Sandwich

20 slices white bread
 1 cup butter
10 thin slices turkey
     salt and pepper to taste

Spread bread slices thinly with butter. Arrange turkey slices neatly on half the bread and season with salt and pepper. Cover with remaining bread.

Yields 40 sandwiches.

Chopped Tongue and Chicken Sandwich

2/3 cup minced cooked chicken
1/3 cup chopped cooked tongue
     butter, softened
     salt to taste
     cayenne pepper to taste
     curry powder to taste
20 thin slices rye bread

In a bowl, combine the chicken and tongue and work in enough butter to make a paste. Season with salt, cayenne, and curry powder. Assemble sandwiches.

Yields 40 sandwiches.

Chicken, Ham, and Walnut Tea Sandwich

  1 cup ground chicken
1/2 cup ground walnuts
1/4 cup ground ham
1/4 cup butter
  2 tablespoons heavy cream
  2 teaspoons minced parsley
    salt and pepper to taste
20 thin slices whole wheat bread

In a bowl, combine the chicken, walnuts, ham, butter, cream, parsley, salt, and pepper. Mix well and assemble sandwiches.

Yields 40 sandwiches.

Westphalian Ham Fingers

1/2 cup mayonnaise
  3 tablespoons minced pitted green olives
  1 tablespoon minced cornichons
  1 tablespoon minced parsley
  1 tablespoon minced scallion
  2 teaspoons Dijon mustard
    salt and pepper to taste
14 very thin slices pumpernickel
1/2 pound Westphalian ham, thinly sliced
  1 bunch watercress

In a bowl, combine the mayonnaise, olives, cornichons, parsley, scallion, mustard, salt, and pepper. Spread bread slices with mayonnaise mixture. Divide the ham among half the bread slices. Strip leaves from watercress and arrange leaves on ham. Cover with remaining bread slices.

Yields about 28 sandwiches.

6 Tea Sandwiches

Apricot Ham Sandwich

8 very thin slices white bread

2 tablespoons butter

1/4 teaspoon dry mustard

2 tablespoons apricot jam

4 thin slices ham

Cut crusts from bread and place four slices on a work surface. Mix the butter and mustard and spread thinly on the bread. Spread jam on the butter and place a ham slice on each. Cover with remaining bread slices.

Yields about 16 sandwiches.

Ham and Cheese Finger Rolls

6 finger rolls

2 tablespoons hot milk

1/4 cup grated cheddar cheese

1/2 cup minced cooked ham

butter

Preheat oven to 300°F.

Split rolls almost in half lengthwise. Scoop out soft center crumb.

In a bowl, combine the crumb, milk, cheese, and ham. Mix well. Stuff the rolls with the cheese mixture. Place on a baking sheet and brush rolls with butter. Bake 15 minutes or until lightly toasted and heated through.

Yields 6 sandwiches.

Chapter 7

Open-Faced Sandwiches

These wonderful sandwiches are as good for business as an attractively displayed dessert table. People "eat" with their eyes first, and an assortment of beautifully prepared sandwiches is difficult to resist. It is possible that your customers will try more than one.

Although the Scandinavians are given credit for the open-faced sandwich, other nations have served foods attractively on a single slice of bread. Wherever the source, the most important features of these sandwiches are their careful preparation and attractive presentation. The sandwiches

Egg and Radish Sandwich

2 hard-cooked eggs, chopped
1 tablespoon minced scallion
1 tablespoon grated cheddar cheese
3 tablespoons mayonnaise
2 crusty rolls
3 radishes, thinly sliced

Combine the eggs, scallion, cheese, and mayonnaise and mix well. Spread on rolls, garnish with radishes, and serve open-faced.

Yields 2 sandwiches.

should be assembled to order, if at all possible, or made within an hour before serving. One way to prepare them ahead so the bread won't become soggy is to arrange all of the ingredients (except the bread) on baking sheets and hold them in the refrigerator. When required, scoop up the entire sandwich with a broad spatula and transfer to the bread. However, these ingredients can only be held for about an hour or they will lose their crisp and fresh appearance. Their flavor will be best if they can be served at just below room temperature.

The bread must be solid and firmly textured. Flimsy, puffy commercial breads will not hold up with these fillings. Inappropriate breads will turn these delicious sandwiches into unacceptable meals.

Open-faced sandwiches belie the rule of keeping ingredients carefully within the confines of the bread. Often the slices of food are purposely arranged to drape over the edges of the bread. These sandwiches are always carefully garnished (see photographs).

Egg and Tomato Sandwich

   1 slice pumpernickel
1-1/2 teaspoons anchovy butter
     lettuce leaves
   1 hard-cooked egg, sliced
   3 thin slices tomato
     minced chive

Spread pumpernickel with anchovy butter and arrange lettuce on top. Add egg and tomato slices and sprinkle with chives.

Yields 1 sandwich.

Herring Sandwich

     lettuce leaves
   1 slice rye bread, buttered
   3 pieces pickled herring
2 or 3 onion rings
   1 tomato wedge

Arrange lettuce on the bread and top with herring. Garnish with onion rings and tomato.

Yields 1 sandwich.

Lobster Sandwich

1 pound cooked lobster meat, cut in chunks
1/2 cup mayonnaise
1 tablespoon lemon juice
1 teaspoon dry mustard
1/2 teaspoon Worcestershire sauce
Tabasco sauce to taste
8 to 10 slices white bread
mayonnaise
Boston lettuce leaves
capers

In a bowl, combine the lobster, 1/2 cup mayonnaise, lemon juice, mustard, Worcestershire, and Tabasco.

Toast bread on one side and remove crusts. Spread untoasted sides with mayonnaise and arrange a lettuce leaf neatly on top. Place lobster mixture on lettuce and garnish with capers.

Yields 8 to 10 sandwiches.

Smoked Salmon Sandwich

3 slices smoked salmon
1 slice rye bread, buttered
1/2 cup cold scrambled egg
1 tablespoon salmon caviar
minced chives

Arrange salmon slices on bread. Form a diagonal strip of egg across the salmon. Place caviar on one side of the egg and chives on the other.

Yields 1 sandwich.

7 **Open-Faced Sandwiches**

Wined Sardine Sandwich

2 tablespoons butter

1 small onion, minced

2 garlic cloves, crushed

1 3-inch strip lemon peel

1 cup dry white wine

1 bay leaf

2 3-3/4-ounce cans sardines

6 slices toast, buttered

1 cup sliced mushrooms, sauteed

In a skillet, melt the butter and saute onion and garlic until soft but not brown. Add the lemon peel, wine, and bay leaf and simmer 10 minutes.

Drain the oil from the sardines and arrange them in a flat dish. Pour the hot marinade over and let stand for 1 hour or longer.

Drain the sardines, arrange on toast slices, and scatter mushrooms on top.

Yields 6 sandwiches.

Shrimp Sandwich

lettuce leaves

1 slice white bread, buttered

1 cup tiny shrimp, cooked, peeled, and deveined

lemon wedges

Arrange lettuce on the bread and cover with neatly arranged shrimp. Garnish with lemon wedges.

Yields 1 sandwich.

Shrimp and Egg Sandwich

1/3 cup butter

2 tablespoons mayonnaise

1 teaspoon minced dill

Tabasco sauce to taste

salt to taste

6 slices whole grain rye bread

2 hard-cooked eggs, sliced

24 sprigs watercress

1-1/2 pounds shrimp, cooked, peeled, and deveined

red caviar

minced dill

In a bowl, cream the butter. Beat in the mayonnaise, dill, Tabasco, and salt. Spread the bread with butter. Arrange a diagonal row of egg slices on the bread. Place watercress on one triangle of bread and arrange shrimp neatly on remaining triangle. Garnish with caviar and dill.

Yields 6 sandwiches.

Shrimp, Tuna, and Green Bean Sandwich

1 ounce shrimp, chopped

1 ounce dark tuna, flaked

1 teaspoon minced celery

1 tablespoon mayonnaise

1/2 teaspoon lemon juice

1 slice dark rye bread, buttered

1/4 cup sliced marinated mushrooms

6 marinated green beans

3 slices hard-cooked egg

In a bowl, combine the shrimp, tuna, celery, mayonnaise, and lemon juice. Spread mixture on the bread. Arrange mushrooms and beans on top and garnish with egg.

Yields 1 sandwich.

Shrimp and Turkey Sandwich

4 slices dark rye bread or pumpernickel
6 tablespoons curry butter
1/2 pound cooked turkey breast, sliced
16 shrimp, cooked and shelled
4 hard-cooked eggs, sliced
5 red radishes, thinly sliced
1 cucumber, thinly sliced
1 avocado
1 tablespoon grated onion
4 ounces cream cheese
1 tablespoon sour cream
lemon juice to taste
Tabasco sauce to taste
dill sprigs

Butter the bread with curry butter. Arrange the turkey, shrimp, eggs, radishes, and cucumbers on the bread.

In a processor, puree the avocado with the onion, cream cheese, sour cream, lemon juice, and Tabasco. Pipe onto the sandwiches and garnish with dill sprigs.

Yields 4 sandwiches.

Chicken Sandwich Remoulade

1 large slice dark rye bread
escarole leaf
2 tablespoons shredded iceberg lettuce
3 tablespoons Remoulade sauce
1 large slice Gruyere cheese
2 large slices chicken breast
2 slices crisp bacon
1 tablespoon chopped hard-cooked egg
3 slices green olive
2 tomato quarters

Cover the bread with escarole and sprinkle with shredded lettuce. Spread 1 tablespoon Remoulade sauce over lettuce and arrange cheese and chicken on top. Place bacon on chicken and sprinkle with egg. Garnish with olive, tomato, and remaining remoulade sauce.

Yields 1 sandwich.

Turkey Sandwich

2 slices white bread, toasted
  butter
4 lettuce leaves
2 or 3 slices tomato
3 or 4 thin slices cooked turkey
3 or 4 tablespoons Lamaze dressing
  (see following recipe)
4 or 5 strips crisp bacon

Spread toast slices with butter. Arrange lettuce leaves on toast. Top one toast with tomato and the other with turkey. Ladle dressing over both slices and arrange bacon strips on top.

Yields 1 sandwich.

Lamaze Dressing

1 cup chili sauce
1 cup mayonnaise
1/4 cup minced chutney
1 hard-cooked egg, chopped
2 tablespoons minced celery
1 tablespoon A-1 sauce
1 teaspoon minced chives
1 teaspoon minced pimiento
1 teaspoon minced green pepper
  salt and pepper to taste
  paprika to taste

In a bowl, combine the chili sauce, mayonnaise, and chutney. Stir in the egg, celery, and A-1 sauce. Add the chives, pimiento, green pepper, salt, pepper, and paprika. Cover and chill for 2 hours before serving.

Yields about 2-1/2 cups.

Note: Dressing will keep 4 days in the refrigerator. Use for sandwiches or a seafood dip.

Roast Beef Sandwich

2 slices rare roast beef
1 slice rye bread, buttered
1 slice Danish blue cheese
2 slices mustard pickle
1 gherkin fan

Arrange beef slices on bread and place cheese in the center. Arrange mustard pickles around the cheese and the gherkin fan on top.

Yields 1 sandwich.

English Beef and Cheese Sandwich

2 teaspoons cream cheese, softened
2 teaspoons crumbled blue cheese
1 slice pumpernickel, buttered
2 ounces roast beef, thinly sliced
  salt and pepper to taste
3 slices pickled beets
2 herring fillets

Mix cheeses together and spread on the bread. Arrange beef on top and season with salt and pepper. Garnish with beets and herring.

Yields 1 sandwich.

Frikadeller Sandwich

1 to 2 cold meatballs, sliced
  (preferably veal)
1 slice rye bread, buttered
2 tablespoons grated pickled beets
  cucumber slices

Arrange meatball slices on bread and garnish with beets and cucumber.

Yields 1 sandwich.

Roast Pork Sandwich

3 slices cold roast pork
1 slice rye bread, buttered
1 tablespoon pork cracklings (see note)
2 prunes, soaked in orange juice
1 slice orange
  grated gingerroot

Arrange pork slices on bread and sprinkle with cracklings. Place prunes on meat and separate by curling an orange slice around them. Sprinkle with gingerroot.

Yields 1 sandwich.

Note: For pork cracklings, finely dice 2 tablespoons minced salt pork and cook over low heat in a small skillet until golden and crisp. Drain on paper towels. Discard liquid fat.

Ham and Shrimp Sandwich

1-1/2 tablespoons butter
1/4 cup cooked shrimp, chopped
1 teaspoon crumbled blue cheese
1/2 teaspoon minced parsley
lemon juice to taste
1/4 teaspoon anchovy paste
cayenne pepper to taste
1 slice dark rye bread
3 thin slices baked ham
3 thin slices Gruyere cheese
3 large ripe pitted olives
4 cooked shrimp, peeled and deveined

In a bowl, combine the butter, 1/4 cup shrimp, cheese, parsley, lemon juice, anchovy paste, and cayenne. Spread mixture on the bread.

Use ham and cheese slices together to form three cornucopias and put an olive into each. Arrange on top of shrimp mixture. Arrange a shrimp at the end of each cornucopia and place one in the center of the grouping.

Yields 1 sandwich.

Bacon and Pate Sandwich

3 slices crisp bacon
1 slice rye bread, buttered
1/2 tomato, thinly sliced
2 slices Danish pate (see following recipe)
1 tablespoon minced aspic
grated horseradish

Arrange bacon slices on the bread alternately with tomato slices. Place pate slices on top. Garnish with aspic and sprinkle with horseradish.

Yields 1 sandwich.

7 Open-Faced Sandwiches

Danish Liver Pate

1 pound pork or calves liver, chopped
2 medium onions, chopped
1 pound pork fat, chopped
1/4 cup cognac
   salt and pepper to taste

Preheat oven to 325° F.

In a processor, puree the liver, onions, and pork fat in batches. Place in a bowl and mix in the cognac, salt, and pepper. Mix well. (For a smoother texture, force through a sieve.) Place in a 1-quart loaf pan and bake for 1 hour, or until a thermometer registers 165° F.

Cool and chill for at least 12 hours. Unmold and cut into thin slices.

Yields about 18 slices.

Chicken Liver and Apple Sandwich

1 pound chicken livers
6 tablespoons butter
   salt and pepper to taste
1 onion, thinly sliced
1 golden Delicious apple, peeled and sliced
4 slices whole wheat bread, buttered
2 hard-cooked eggs, thinly sliced

In a skillet, saute the livers in 4 tablespoons butter until browned but still pink in the center. Season with salt and pepper. Transfer livers to a plate with a slotted spoon.

In the skillet, saute the onion until soft and lightly browned. Drain and set aside. Saute the apple in remaining butter until crisp tender.

Cut livers into thin slices and arrange on bread. Top with onion, apple, and egg.

Yields 4 sandwiches.

Chapter 8
Canapes & Toasts

Many restaurateurs are learning that giving something away can increase their business noticeably. Most restaurants have only a few minutes to win the confidence and approval of their guests. A properly trained staff will see that guests have a cocktail within a few minutes of being seated, and a knowledgeable owner will provide something to eat at the same time. The guest who is kept waiting for that first drink and something to nibble may not return.

Nuts, chips, or pasty cheese mixtures were once acceptable. But now that diners' tastes are more

Canapes Nicoises
Tomato-Olive Canapes

    32 bread rounds
        butter
   1/2 cup anchovy butter
 1-1/2 cups minced, drained tomato
    16 black olives, pitted and halved
        minced parsley

Saute bread rounds in butter until golden on both sides. Drain and let cool.

Spread the rounds with anchovy butter and arrange the tomato on top. Top each with an olive half. Garnish edges with parsley.

Yields 32 canapes.

sophisticated, owners must offer more varied and interesting foods to overcome their competition. A selection of carefully chosen and prepared canapes or toasts to be served with cocktails, either gratis or at a small charge, can create a favorable atmosphere that in turn will encourage your guests to relax and spend even more time (and money) in your restaurant. The cost of ingredients is negligible, and this is often a way of using leftovers inventively.

If canapes have been denigrated, it is because often they are not given the care and attention required. They should be freshly made and not only delicious to eat but also appealing to the eye. Three or four served to each guest on a doily-lined plate, or a large tray offered to each diner, can enhance the image of your dining room.

The chef should organize the staff into an assembly line to prepare canapes and toasts as quickly and efficiently as possible. They must be prepared shortly before serving or the bread or toast will be limp or soggy. If you wish, coat the canapes with aspic to make them sparkle and to keep the ingredients from drying out. However, if made too far ahead, even aspic-coated canapes become limp.

Roquefort Radish Canapes

4 ounces Roquefort cheese

4 ounces butter

8 slices bread

   radishes, thinly sliced

   parsley sprigs

Combine the cheese and butter and spread on bread slices. Cut into shapes and garnish each with radish and parsley.

Yields 32 canapes.

Mushroom Canapes

8 slices bread

1/4 cup marjoram butter

1/2 pound marinated mushrooms, thinly sliced

   lemon rind, finely shredded

Spread bread slices with the butter and cut into fingers. Arrange mushrooms in overlapping slices on the bread and garnish with lemon rind.

Yields 32 canapes.

The following recipes do not always suggest a particular type of bread because many types can be used. Some, however, indicate the best bread for flavor and texture. Canapes are always cut into small shapes about 1-1/2 to 2-1/2 inches in size. They can be squares, rounds, crescents, diagonals, rectangles, or other decorative shapes made with cutters. Toasts are hot canapes that must be served immediately after heating. Do not assemble them too far in advance or the filling will make the toast base soggy.

Spinach Onion-Ring Canapes

8 slices bread
  butter
1/4 cup nutmeg butter
2 pounds cooked spinach, drained
  salt and pepper to taste
  fried onion rings

Cut bread into shapes and saute in butter until golden. Drain and spread with nutmeg butter.

Mince the spinach and season with salt and pepper. Arrange on canapes and garnish with onion rings.

Yields 32 canapes.

Shrimp Canapes

8 slices bread

1/4 cup dill butter

32 large shrimp

2 hard-cooked egg yolks, sieved
dill sprigs

Spread the bread with dill butter and cut into rounds or crescents to fit shrimp. Place a shrimp on each and garnish with egg and dill.

Yields 32 canapes.

Smoked Salmon Canapes

8 slices bread

1/4 cup horseradish butter
thin slices smoked salmon
tiny raw onion rings
capers

Spread bread slices with horseradish butter and arrange smoked salmon to fit the bread. Cut into shapes and garnish with onion and capers.

Yields 32 canapes.

Canapes a la Hongroise

Chicken and Paprika Butter Canapes

1/4 pound butter

1 teaspoon paprika

8 slices white bread

2 cups minced chicken
mayonnaise to taste
salt and pepper to taste
red and green pepper, julienne

In a bowl, combine the butter and paprika and mix well. Spread on the bread.

In another bowl, combine the chicken, enough mayonnaise to bind, and salt and pepper. Spread on bread and cut into shapes. Garnish with julienned pepper.

Yields 32 canapes.

Chicken Liver Canapes

1 pound chicken livers
3 cups chicken stock
2 hard-cooked eggs
1/4 cup minced onion
2 tablespoons butter
8 slices white bread
   salt and pepper to taste
   minced parsley

In a saucepan, simmer the chicken livers in stock until just barely pink in the center, about 10 minutes. Drain. (You can clarify this liquid and make aspic, if desired.) In a processor, puree livers and eggs.

Saute the onion in butter until soft, but not brown, and puree with the livers. Season with salt and pepper.

Toast the bread on one side only and spread untoasted sides with the liver mixture. Cut into shapes and sprinkle edges with parsley. Coat with aspic if desired.

Yields 32 canapes.

Steak Tartare Canapes

1 pound sirloin, finely chopped
1/4 cup minced onion
2 egg yolks
   salt and pepper to taste
32 bread squares, sauteed in butter
32 anchovy fillets, rolled
   capers
   minced parsley

In a bowl, combine the sirloin, onion, egg yolks, salt, and pepper. Mix well. Spread thickly on bread squares. Garnish with anchovies, capers, and parsley.

Yields 32 canapes.

Salami Canapes

8 slices pumpernickel
1/2 cup butter, softened
   salami, thinly sliced

Spread the bread sparingly with butter and cover evenly with salami. Cut into shapes and garnish with butter put through a pastry bag.

Yields 32 canapes.

8 Canapes & Toasts

Ham and Mustard Canapes

8 slices bread
butter
1/4 cup mustard butter
8 thin slices boiled ham
32 slices mustard pickle

Cut the bread into shapes and saute in butter on both sides until golden. Drain. Spread bread with the mustard butter and top with ham cut to fit. Garnish with mustard pickle.

Yields 32 canapes.

Croutes au Fromage
Baked Cheese Sandwiches

1-1/4 cups flour
dash of salt
dash of cayenne pepper
1 cup grated cheddar cheese
6 tablespoons butter
3 tablespoons heavy cream
1 egg, lightly beaten
1 cup grated Gruyere cheese
2 tablespoons butter, softened

Preheat oven to 450° F.

In a bowl, combine the flour, salt, and cayenne and mix well. Work in the cheddar cheese and 6 tablespoons butter until it forms a coarse meal. Stir in the cream and shape into a flat cake. Chill 30 minutes.

Roll the dough 1/4 inch thick on a lightly floured board. Cut into 1-inch circles. Place on an unbuttered baking sheet and brush rounds with egg. Bake 6 to 8 minutes until lightly browned.

Cream Gruyere and remaining butter together. Spread on half the rounds, top with remaining rounds, and warm in the oven.

Yields about 40 toasts.

Croutes a la Lorraine

Cheese Toasts

    20 slices French bread, 1/4 inch
        thick
    1/2 cup butter
      3 eggs, lightly beaten
      5 slices crisp bacon, crumbled
      1 cup grated Gruyere cheese

Preheat oven to 400° F.

In a skillet, saute the bread in butter until golden on both sides. Combine the eggs, bacon, and cheese. Spread mixture on the bread. Bake for 10 minutes or until golden.

Yields 24 toasts.

Onion and Cheese Toasts

      6 club rolls
    1/2 cup butter
      3 tablespoons Dijon mustard
    1/4 teaspoon cayenne pepper
      6 ounces cheddar cheese, thinly
         sliced
      1 onion, thinly sliced

Preheat oven to 350° F.

Slice each roll into 1/2-inch thick slices. In a bowl, combine the butter, mustard, and cayenne. Spread on the slices and add a layer of cheese and onion. Bake for 15 minutes.

Yields 24 to 32 toasts.

8 Canapes & Toasts

97

Dutch Toasts

1/2 pound finnan haddie

2 tablespoons butter

3/4 cup hot Bechamel sauce

12 toast rounds

12 slices hard-cooked egg

Mince the haddock and saute in butter until flaky. Fold in the sauce and spread on toast rounds. Garnish with egg and serve hot.

Yields 12 toasts.

Grilled Lobster Toasts

1/2 cup Bechamel sauce

1-1/2 teaspoons tomato paste

1 teaspoon lemon juice

1-1/2 cups cooked lobster

6 slices white bread

6 tablespoons grated Gruyere cheese

Preheat broiler.

Reduce Bechamel to 1/3 cup and stir in tomato paste, lemon juice, and lobster. Cut each bread slice into four rounds and toast on one side.

Spread untoasted sides with lobster mixture and sprinkle with cheese. Brown under the broiler.

Yields 24 toasts.

Croutes a la Dieppe

Dieppe Toasts

8 slices bread

butter

32 mussels, cooked and shelled

beurre blanc (see Chapter 11)

Preheat oven to 400° F.

Cut the bread into 32 small slices and saute in butter until golden. Arrange mussels on the toasts and coat with beurre blanc. Heat in the oven and serve hot.

Yields 32 toasts.

Crevettes Canapes

Shrimp Toasts

- 8 slices bread
- butter
- 32 shrimp, cooked, peeled, and deveined
- 3/4 cup mustard Hollandaise (see Chapter 11)

Preheat oven to 400° F.

Cut the bread into 32 crescents and saute in butter until golden. Arrange a shrimp on each crescent and coat with Hollandaise. Heat in the oven and serve hot.

Yields 32 toasts.

Chicken and Grape Toasts

- 8 slices bread
- 1 cup minced chicken
- 1/2 cup green grapes, chopped
- 3/4 cup Bechamel sauce
- 1/2 cup grated Gruyere cheese

Preheat broiler.

Cut the bread into 32 shapes and toast on one side. Combine the chicken, grapes, and Bechamel. Spread on untoasted sides of the bread and sprinkle with cheese. Brown under the broiler.

Yields 32 toasts.

Derby Toasts

12 walnut halves
1 cup ground ham
1/2 cup hot Bechamel sauce
  cayenne pepper to taste
3 slices bread, toasted on one side

Preheat oven to 400°F.

Warm walnut halves in the oven. Fold together the ham and Bechamel. Season with cayenne.

Cut each bread slice into four sections and toast on one side. Spread untoasted sides with the ham mixture. Garnish with a walnut half and serve hot.

Yields 12 toasts.

Croutes a la Gayolle
Gayolle Toasts

1/2 cup minced ham
1/2 cup minced sauteed mushrooms
1/2 cup grated Gruyere cheese
1/2 cup Bechamel sauce
  cayenne pepper to taste
8 slices bread

Preheat oven to 400°F.

In a bowl, combine the ham, mushrooms, and cheese with enough Bechamel to bind. Season with cayenne.

Toast the bread on one side and spread untoasted sides with ham mixture. Cut into shapes. Heat in the oven and serve hot.

Yields 32 toasts.

Chapter 9

Croque-Monsieur, Pain Perdu, or French Toast Sandwiches

Pain perdu, literally "lost bread," or French toast sandwiches are assembled, dipped in an egg wash, and sauteed or deep fried. In recent years, they have become very popular not only as lunch offerings but also for breakfast or supper. Croque-monsieur (a sauteed ham and cheese sandwich) is one of the more common versions.

Many of the sandwiches in other chapters can be prepared in this manner to add interest to your menu. They are particularly suited to the needs of chefs who cater to conventions or work in cafeterias. The sandwiches can be assembled

Mozzarella in Carozza

> 6 slices thin bread
> 3 1/4-inch thick slices mozzarella cheese
> 2 eggs, lightly beaten
> oil for deep frying
> 1/2 cup butter
> 6 anchovy fillets, chopped
> 1 tablespoon minced parsley

Make sandwiches of bread and cheese and cut into rounds or ovals. Dip in the egg and let excess drain off.

Heat oil to 375° F. and fry sandwiches until golden.

In a saucepan, heat butter until golden. Stir in the anchovy fillets and parsley. Serve as a dipping sauce for the sandwiches.

Yields 3 sandwiches.

ahead of time and dipped in the egg mixture shortly before cooking. Although not at their best, they can be held in a warm oven for up to 30 minutes before serving.

The small restaurant may want to invest in special molds designed to compress the sandwich and give it a particular form. Molds are available from gourmet shops and restaurant suppliers.

Innovative chefs will recognize the infinite possibilities for filling the sandwiches. Try using cheeses such as chevre or blue, instead of the traditional Gruyere, and vary the meats from ham and chicken to salami and shrimp.

Grilled Shrimp Sandwich

    5 ounces cooked shrimp, chopped
  1/2 cup minced celery
    1 teaspoon minced onion
  1/2 teaspoon salt
  1/2 teaspoon chili powder
  1/4 teaspoon crushed garlic
  1/4 teaspoon ground pepper
  1/4 cup mayonnaise
   10 slices bread, buttered
    3 eggs, lightly beaten
    3 tablespoons milk
  1/4 teaspoon salt
      butter

In a bowl, combine the shrimp, celery, onion, 1/2 teaspoon salt, chili powder, garlic, pepper, and mayonnaise. Spread on half the bread slices and cover with remaining slices.

In a bowl, combine the eggs, milk, and remaining salt. Dip sandwiches in the egg mixture and saute in butter.

Yields 5 sandwiches.

Sausage and Cheese Pain Perdu

1 cup flour
1 teaspoon baking powder
1-1/4 teaspoons salt
2 eggs, lightly beaten
1-1/2 cups beer
2 tablespoons butter
1/2 cup minced onion
1/2 pound breakfast sausage, minced
1/4 pound bacon, crumbled
4 ounces cream cheese
1/2 teaspoon pepper
20 1/2-inch-thick slices bread
1-1/2 cups vegetable oil
1-1/2 tablespoons paprika

In a bowl, combine the flour, baking powder, and 1 teaspoon salt. Stir in the eggs and slowly work in the beer to make a smooth batter. Let stand, covered, for at least 2 hours.

In a skillet, melt the butter and saute onion and sausage until the onion is soft, but not brown. Drain off the fat. In a bowl, combine the onion, sausage, bacon, cream cheese, remaining salt, and pepper and mix well. Chill until ready to use.

Heat oil to 375° F. Assemble sandwiches and dip in the batter. Fry until golden. Drain and sprinkle with paprika before serving.

Yields 10 sandwiches.

9 *Croque-Monsieur, Pain Perdu, —or— French Toast Sandwiches*

Sauteed Tomato and Cheese Sandwich

2 tomatoes, peeled and seeded

1/2 cup sour cream

1/2 cup grated Gruyere cheese

2 tablespoons minced dill

2 tablespoons minced chives

lemon juice to taste

salt and pepper to taste

8 thin slices white bread, crusts removed

butter

2 eggs

1/4 cup milk

clarified butter

Slice tomatoes 1/4 inch thick and set aside. Combine the sour cream, cheese, dill, chives, lemon juice, salt, and pepper. Butter one side of each bread slice. Spread cheese mixture on the buttered side of half the slices, leaving a 1/4-inch border.

Arrange tomato slices on top and cover with remaining bread slices buttered side down. Beat eggs and milk together and season with salt and pepper. Dip sandwiches in the egg mixture and saute in clarified butter until golden on each side.

Yields 4 sandwiches.

Pain Perdu a la Reine

French Toast with Chicken

4 eggs
1 cup milk
1/2 teaspoon salt
pinch of cayenne pepper
6 3/4-inch-thick slices bread
6 boneless chicken breasts, halved
6 tablespoons butter
salt and pepper to taste
6 tablespoons butter
2 cups Mornay sauce
1/2 cup grated Gruyere cheese

Preheat oven to 375°F.

Beat eggs with the milk and season with 1/2 teaspoon salt and cayenne. Soak bread slices in the egg mixture.

Bake the chicken breasts in one layer with 6 tablespoons butter and season with salt and pepper until just cooked, about 10 to 12 minutes.

Cut bread slices diagonally and saute in remaining butter until golden. Arrange bread and chicken alternately on a heatproof platter and coat with sauce. Sprinkle with cheese and glaze under the broiler.

Yields 6 sandwiches.

Milwaukee Sandwich

thin slices cooked chicken
2 slices white bread
1 teaspoon crumbled Roquefort cheese
paprika to taste
butter
parsley

Place chicken on one bread slice and sprinkle with cheese and paprika. Place remaining bread slice on top and butter outside of sandwich. Grill on both sides until golden. Serve with parsley.

Yields 1 sandwich.

9 *Croque-Monsieur, Pain Perdu, —or— French Toast Sandwiches*

105

Monte Cristo Sandwich

butter
2 slices white bread, crusts removed
1 thin slice baked ham
2 thin slices cooked chicken
1 thin slice Gruyere cheese
1 egg, lightly beaten
currant jelly, optional

Butter a slice of bread. Top with ham, chicken, cheese, and remaining slice of bread.

Dip into the egg and saute in additional butter until golden on both sides. Serve with currant jelly on the side.

Yields 1 sandwich.

Croque-Monsieur

2 slices bread, buttered
1 thin slice baked ham
1 thin slice Gruyere cheese
1 egg, lightly beaten
butter

Make a sandwich with the bread, ham, and cheese. Dip sandwich in the egg and saute in butter until golden.

Yields 1 sandwich.

Ham, Egg, and Pepper Croque-Monsieur

1 cup chopped ham
2 hard-cooked eggs, minced
2 tablespoons minced green pepper
2 tablespoons minced sour pickle
  mayonnaise
8 slices bread
1 egg, lightly beaten
1/2 cup milk
  butter

In a bowl, combine the ham, eggs, pepper, and pickle. Add enough mayonnaise to bind. Spread the mixture on half the bread slices and cover with remaining slices.

Combine the egg and milk. Dip sandwiches in the egg mixture and saute in butter until golden on both sides.

Yields 4 sandwiches.

9 Croque-Monsieur, Pain Perdu, —or— French Toast Sandwiches

Chapter 10

International Sandwiches

The following recipes may not qualify as sandwiches in the usual sense, but they achieve the same results when included on a menu. They are intriguing enough to boost sales, yet not so different as to discourage the customers. Try some occasionally and see if they are popular enough to become permanent additions.

Offering turnovers from Latin America or Dim Sum from China can distinguish your dining room from the competition. These recipes in general are easy and do not require any special equipment.

Eggplant and Cheese Sandwich

    1 pound peeled eggplant, cut in 8 1/4-inch-thick slices
      salt
    1 cup bread crumbs
  3/4 cup grated mozzarella cheese
    2 tablespoons grated Parmesan cheese
  1/4 cup minced prosciutto
    2 egg yolks
  1/4 teaspoon dried basil
      salt and pepper to taste
  1/2 cup oil
      flour
    2 eggs, lightly beaten
      bread crumbs
      oil for deep frying

Sprinkle the eggplant with salt and drain for 30 minutes.

In a bowl, combine 1 cup bread crumbs, cheeses, prosciutto, egg yolks, basil, salt, and pepper. Set aside.

Dry eggplant with paper towels. Saute

(Continued on next page)

in a skillet in the oil until browned and tender. Transfer to paper towels.

Spread four eggplant slices with the cheese mixture and top with remaining slices. Dust sandwiches with flour, dip in eggs, and then in bread crumbs. Chill on a rack for 30 minutes.

Heat oil to 375° F. and fry sandwiches until golden.

Yields 4 sandwiches.

Calzone

1 recipe pizza dough (see Chapter 11)
1/2 pound goat cheese
1/4 pound mozzarella cheese, cubed
1/4 cup ricotta cheese
1/2 cup diced prosciutto
1/4 cup grated Parmesan cheese
1/4 teaspoon minced rosemary
1 tablespoon minced basil
2 tablespoons minced parsley
  pepper to taste
2 eggs, lightly beaten
1 tablespoon water

Prepare pizza dough and divide into four portions. Shape into balls, cover, and set aside.

Preheat oven to 400° F.

In a bowl, combine goat cheese, mozzarella, ricotta, prosciutto, Parmesan, rosemary, basil, parsley, pepper, and eggs. Mix well.

Roll each ball of dough into an 8-1/2-inch circle. Spoon one-quarter of the filling on half of each circle. Shape into turnovers and seal edges. Arrange on a baking sheet and let rise 20 minutes. Cut a steam vent in each and brush with water. Bake for 30 minutes.

Yields 4 turnovers.

Note: These can also be deep fried.

Calzone with Ricotta, Tomato, and Mushrooms

- 1 recipe pizza dough
- 1 7-ounce tomato, peeled, seeded, and diced
- 3/4 teaspoon salt
- 1/4 pound mushrooms, thinly sliced
- 1-1/4 cups ricotta cheese
- 1/4 pound mozzarella cheese, grated
- 1/4 pound fontina cheese, grated
- 1/4 cup grated Parmesan cheese
- 2 ounces prosciutto, minced
- 1 garlic clove, minced
- 1 tablespoon basil, minced
  olive oil
- 2 tablespoons grated Parmesan cheese

Preheat oven to 425°F.

Prepare dough and let rise.

Season tomato with salt and drain in a colander for 30 minutes. Squeeze out excess moisture. In a towel, squeeze excess moisture from mushrooms.

Combine ricotta, mozzarella, fontina, 1/4 cup Parmesan, prosciutto, garlic, basil, tomato, and mushrooms and mix well.

Shape pizza dough into four 8-inch circles. Fill half of each circle with stuffing. Brush edges with olive oil and seal. Cut a steam vent in the top. Let rise for 20 minutes. Brush with oil and dust with remaining Parmesan. Bake 30 minutes. Brush with oil again and let rest 5 minutes before serving.

Yields 4 turnovers.

10
International Sandwiches

Picnic Turnovers

2 tablespoons butter
1/2 cup minced mushrooms
   milk
1 tablespoon oil
4 ounces Canadian bacon, diced
1 onion, minced
2 tablespoons butter
3 tablespoons flour
1/4 teaspoon salt
   pepper to taste
   nutmeg to taste
3/4 pound cooked spinach, minced
4 ounces Gruyere cheese, diced
1 recipe pizza dough
1 egg
1 tablespoon milk

Preheat oven to 425° F.

In a skillet, saute mushrooms in butter until they give off their liquid. Drain the juices into a 1-cup measure and add enough milk to make 1 cup. Set aside.

Heat 1 tablespoon oil in a skillet and saute bacon until just cooked. In a skillet, saute the onion in butter until soft. Stir in the flour and cook, stirring, until it just starts to turn golden. Pour in the milk mixture and cook, stirring, until thick and smooth.

Correct seasoning with salt, pepper, and nutmeg. Fold in the mushrooms, bacon, spinach, and cheese. Cover and let cool.

Divide pizza dough into four sections and roll into 12-by-12-inch squares. Divide filling among the squares, forming turnovers. Transfer to a baking sheet, cut a steam vent in each, and brush with a mixture of the egg and 1 tablespoon milk. Let rise 20 minutes, brush with egg mixture again, and bake for 25 minutes.

Yields 4 turnovers.

Sauerkraut Turnovers

2 tablespoons minced onion

1 tablespoon butter

1 cup cooked sauerkraut

1/2 cup chopped, cooked beef, pork, or ham

1 teaspoon minced dill pickle

1 teaspoon minced marjoram

1 teaspoon minced thyme

1 teaspoon dill weed

salt and pepper to taste

1 egg

1 teaspoon sour cream

1 pound flaky pastry (see Chapter 11)

Preheat oven to 400°F.

In a skillet, saute the onion in butter until golden. Add the sauerkraut, meat, pickle, marjoram, thyme, dill, salt, and pepper. Mix in the egg and sour cream and cool.

Roll the pastry 1/4 inch thick and cut into 8-inch rounds. Put filling in the center of each round. Form into turnovers, seal edges, and cut a steam vent in each. Put on a baking sheet and bake until golden, about 20 minutes.

Yields about 6 turnovers.

Empanaditas de Queso

Deep-Fried Cheese Turnovers

1/2 cup minced scallion

1/2 teaspoon ground annatto seed

2 tablespoons corn oil

1-1/2 pounds mozzarella cheese, grated

salt and pepper to taste

1 pound flaky pastry

oil for deep frying

In a skillet, saute the scallion and annatto seed in oil until the scallion is soft. Add to the cheese with salt and pepper.

Roll the pastry 1/16 inch thick and cut into 8-inch rounds. Divide the filling among the rounds and shape into turnovers, sealing the edges. Cut a steam vent in each.

Heat the oil to 375°F. and fry the turnovers until golden, about 8 minutes.

Yields 8 turnovers.

10
International Sandwiches

Seafood Turnovers

3/4 cup dry white wine

1/2 teaspoon salt

3 peppercorns

1 small bay leaf

1/4 teaspoon thyme

celery stalk, minced

1 sprig parsley

1 pound raw scallops, shrimp, or mussels

1 tablespoon butter

1 tablespoon flour

1/2 cup heavy cream

1 egg yolk

1 tablespoon minced parsley

1 recipe flaky pastry

1 egg mixed with 1 tablespoon milk

Preheat oven to 400° F.

In a saucepan, combine the wine, salt, peppercorns, bay leaf, thyme, celery, and parsley. Simmer 5 minutes. Add each fish and cook until just done. Remove each fish from broth and cook the next one. Peel shrimp and remove mussels from shells. Mince fish. Strain fish liquor and reduce to 1/2 cup.

In a saucepan, melt the butter, stir in the flour, and cook until the roux just starts to turn golden. Stir in the fish stock and cream and cook until thick and smooth. Stir some of the sauce into the egg yolk to warm it and return to the sauce. Heat, stirring, until it just reaches a boil. Stir in the fish and parsley. Correct the seasoning with salt and pepper. Cool.

Roll the pastry 1/4 inch thick and cut 8- to 10-inch circles. Fill with seafood filling and form turnovers. Brush with egg and milk mixture and bake until golden, about 20 minutes.

Yields about 6 turnovers.

114

Curried Meat Turnovers

1 teaspoon soy sauce

1/2 teaspoon sesame oil

1 teaspoon rice wine

1/2 pound ground beef

1/2 cup chicken broth

2 teaspoons sugar

1 teaspoon salt

1 tablespoon cornstarch

2 tablespoons water

4 tablespoons peanut oil

1/2 cup minced onion

1 tablespoon curry powder

1 pound flaky pastry

egg wash

Preheat oven to 400°F.

In a bowl, conbine the soy sauce, sesame oil, wine, and beef. In another bowl, combine the broth, sugar, and salt. In another bowl, combine the cornstarch and water.

Heat 2 tablespoons of peanut oil in a wok and saute the meat mixture until it separates and changes color. Drain in a sieve. Heat 2 more tablespoons oil in the wok and stir fry onion until soft. Add curry powder and stir fry 30 seconds. Add the broth mixture and meat and bring to a boil.

Stir the cornstarch mixture to reconstitute, if required. Add to the wok and cook, stirring, until thickened. Cool.

Roll the pastry 1/4 inch thick and cut into four 8-inch rounds. Fill and shape into turnovers. Cut a steam vent in each. Place on a baking sheet, brush with egg wash, and bake until golden, about 20 minutes.

Yields 4 turnovers.

Pork and Cabbage Steamed Buns

 3/4 pound lean pork, minced
 1/4 cup minced scallion
   1 cup shredded celery cabbage
 1-1/2 teaspoons minced garlic
   1 teaspoon minced gingerroot
 1/2 teaspoon salt
 1/2 teaspoon rice vinegar
 1/4 teaspoon pepper
 1/2 teaspoon sesame oil
   6 drops hot oil
     Chinese yeast dough (see Chapter 11)
     dipping sauces

In a bowl, combine the pork, scallion, cabbage, garlic, gingerroot, salt, vinegar, pepper, sesame oil, and hot oil.

Roll the pastry about 1/4 inch thick and cut into 6-inch circles. Fill with mixture, pinch ends together to shape into balls, and let rise for 30 minutes. Place in a steamer and steam until the dough is set and the meat cooked, about 30 minutes.

Yields 8 buns.

Shrimp and Pork Steamed Buns

   6 ounces cooked shrimp, chopped
 1/4 cup minced water chestnuts
   1 pound roast pork, minced
   1 egg white
   1 tablespoon dry sherry
   1 tablespoon cornstarch
   2 teaspoons soy sauce
   2 teaspoons minced scallions
   1 teaspoon sesame oil
   1 teaspoon gingerroot
 1/2 teaspoon sugar
 1/4 teaspoon pepper
     Chinese yeast dough
     dipping sauces

In a bowl, combine the shrimp, water chestnuts, pork, egg white, sherry, cornstarch, soy sauce, scallion, sesame oil, gingerroot, sugar, and pepper.

Roll the pastry 1/4 inch thick and cut into 6-inch circles. Fill with mixture, pinch ends to shape into balls, and let rise for 30 minutes. Steam until puffed and cooked through, about 20 minutes.

Yields about 10 buns.

Cha Siu Bao
Roast Pork Steamed Buns

3 tablespoons oyster sauce
3 tablespoons sugar
2 tablespoons light soy sauce
1 tablespoon sesame oil
2 teaspoons flour
2 teaspoons cornstarch
1/3 cup water
2 tablespoons lard
1/2 pound roast pork, 1/4-inch dice
2 tablespoons minced garlic
2 tablespoons minced scallion
Chinese yeast dough

In a bowl, blend the oyster sauce, sugar, soy sauce, and sesame oil. Set aside. In another bowl, combine flour, cornstarch, and water. Set aside.

In a wok, heat the lard and stir fry pork until hot. Add the garlic and scallion and stir fry for 15 seconds. Add the oyster sauce and cook, stirring, for 45 seconds. Stir the cornstarch mixture and add to the wok. Cook, stirring, about 30 seconds until thickened. Cool.

Roll dough 1/4 inch thick and cut into 6-inch circles. Fill, pinch to seal edges, and shape into round balls. Let rise for 20 minutes. Steam until puffed and cooked through, about 15 minutes.

Yields about 12 buns.

10
International Sandwiches

Lamb in Pita Bread with Yogurt Sauce
(See page 8.)

Empanaditas de Queso
Deep-Fried Cheese Turnovers
(See page 113.)

Horseradish Cheese Croute
(See page 13.)

Color Plate 9

**Shrimp and Egg
Sandwich, Lobster
Sandwich, Roast
Beef Sandwich**
*(See pages 85, 83,
and 87.)*

**Open-Faced Flounder
Sandwich**
(See page 17.)

**Cucumber and
Shrimp Sandwich**
(See page 3.)

**Herring Sandwich,
Egg and Radish
Sandwich, Smoked
Salmon Sandwich**
(See pages 81-83.)

Panini Rustici
Rustic Bread
(See page 27.)

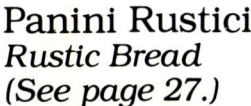

Peacemaker, Poor
Boy, or Oyster Loaf
(See page 57.)

Canapes a la
Hongroise, Spinach
Onion-Ring Canapes,
Canapes Nicoises
*(See pages 94, 93,
and 91.)*

Chapter 11

Basic Sauces, Butters, & Doughs

Although the recipes in this chapter should be in the repertoire of any chef, there are times when our memories need a little prod. We hope that chefs will appreciate our intention and not take offense.

Although it is possible to purchase sauces such as mayonnaise, tartar, and others, they are far superior if made in house. In addition to being easy and quick to prepare, you control the ingredients and can make sure that no additives or excess sugar are used.

Bechamel Sauce

2 tablespoons butter
1 tablespoon minced onion
4 tablespoons flour
3 cups milk, scalded
1/4 teaspoon salt
3 white peppercorns
   sprig of parsley
   pinch of grated nutmeg

In a saucepan, melt the butter and saute the onion until soft but not brown. Stir in the flour and cook until the roux is bubbly and just turning golden. Gradually add the milk, stirring constantly, and cook until thick and smooth.

Season with salt, peppercorns, parsley, and nutmeg. Set over low heat and simmer 30 minutes, or until reduced to two-thirds of the original quantity. Strain.

Yields 2 cups.

Mornay Sauce

3 egg yolks
1/2 cup heavy cream
2 cups hot Bechamel sauce
2 tablespoons butter
2 tablespoons grated Gruyere cheese

In a bowl, combine the egg yolks and cream. Add 1 cup hot Bechamel to warm the egg yolk mixture. Turn the mixture into the remaining Bechamel and cook, stirring constantly, until the sauce just reaches the boiling point. Stir in the butter and cheese.

Yields 2 cups.

Mushroom Duxelles

1/2 pound mushrooms, minced
2 shallots, minced
4 tablespoons butter
salt to taste
2 teaspoons minced parsley

In a skillet, saute the mushrooms and shallots in the butter until the moisture has evaporated. Season with salt and stir in the parsley.

Yields approximately 3/4 cup.

Hollandaise Sauce

3 egg yolks

1 tablespoon water

1/2 cup butter

salt to taste

lemon juice to taste

In a heavy saucepan, combine the egg yolks and water. Whisk, over medium heat, until light and fluffy. Add the butter, one-third at a time, whisking until incorporated. Season with salt and lemon juice.

Yields 1 cup.

Mustard Hollandaise

1 tablespoon Dijon mustard, or to taste

1 cup hot Hollandaise sauce

Fold the mustard into the Hollandaise.

Yields 1 cup.

Beurre Blanc

4 shallots, minced

1 cup white wine vinegar

3/4 cup butter

2 teaspoons minced parsley, optional

salt and pepper to taste

In a saucepan, simmer the shallots and vinegar until reduced to 1/4 cup. Beat in the butter until the sauce mounts. Fold in the parsley, if desired, and salt and pepper.

Yields 1 cup.

Compound Butters

Sandwiches are often spread with butter. The use of flavored or compound butters adds another dimension to your offerings. Many of the recipes in this book suggest a specific flavored butter, but you may select one of your choice. One point to remember is not to mix too many flavors together. Pure butter may be a better accompaniment to many sandwiches.

Anchovy Butter

  1 pound butter
12 anchovy fillets

Work the butter and anchovies together until smooth.

Yields 1 pound.

Curry Butter

1 pound butter
2 tablespoons curry powder, or
   to taste

Work the butter and curry powder together until smooth.

Yields 1 pound.

Dill Butter

   1 pound butter
1/4 teaspoon dill powder
   4 tablespoons minced fresh dill

Work the butter, dill powder, and fresh dill into a smooth paste.

Yields 1 pound.

Horseradish Butter

1 pound butter
4 tablespoons horseradish

Work the butter and horseradish together until smooth.

Yields 1 pound.

Marjoram or Rosemary Butter

1 pound butter

4 teaspoons dried marjoram or rosemary

4 tablespoons minced fresh marjoram or rosemary

In a bowl, work the butter and marjorams together until smooth.

Yields 1 pound.

Mustard Butter

1 pound butter

4 tablespoons Dijon mustard

Work the butter and mustard together until smooth.

Yields 1 pound.

Note: You can substitute 4 teaspoons of dry mustard, or to taste, for the Dijon mustard, or a mixture of the two can be used.

Nutmeg Butter

1 pound butter

2 to 3 tablespoons ground nutmeg

Work the butter and nutmeg together until smooth.

Yields 1 pound.

Dressings

Mayonnaise

2 egg yolks

1/2 teaspoon salt

pinch of white pepper

1/2 teaspoon dry mustard

2 tablespoons vinegar, or to taste

1 cup oil

Beat egg yolks with the salt, pepper, mustard, and vinegar until they start to thicken. While beating, add the oil in a slow, steady stream. Correct seasoning with salt, pepper, and vinegar.

Yields 1-1/2 cups.

Basic
11 *Sauces, Butters, & Doughs*

Remoulade Sauce

2 teaspoons dry mustard
2 teaspoons lemon juice
1 teaspoon capers, minced
2 tablespoons minced dill
1 tablespoon minced parsley
1/2 teaspoon minced garlic
1 hard-cooked egg, minced
2 cups mayonnaise
  salt and cayenne pepper to taste

Combine the mustard and lemon juice. Stir in the capers, dill, parsley, garlic, egg, and mayonnaise. Correct seasoning with salt and cayenne.

Yields 2 cups.

Russian Dressing

2 cups mayonnaise
6 tablespoons chili sauce
2 teaspoons minced pimiento
2 teaspoons minced chives

Combine the mayonnaise, chili sauce, pimiento, and chives.

Yields 2-1/2 cups.

Sauce Tartare

1-1/2 cups mayonnaise
1 dill pickle, minced
2 scallions, minced
1 anchovy fillet, minced
1 teaspoon minced parsley
1 tablespoon capers, minced
2 teaspoons Dijon mustard
1 tablespoon heavy cream
1/2 teaspoon lemon juice
  salt and pepper to taste

Combine the mayonnaise, pickle, scallions, anchovy, parsley, capers, Dijon mustard, cream, lemon juice, and salt and pepper to taste.

Yields 2 cups.

Vinaigrette

2 tablespoons vinegar or lemon juice
2 teaspoons Dijon mustard
1/4 teaspoon salt
   pinch of pepper
1/2 cup olive oil

Combine the vinegar, mustard, salt, pepper, and oil and mix well.
Yields 1/2 cup.

Tomato Coulis

6 cups peeled, seeded, and chopped tomatoes
4 tablespoons butter
   salt and pepper to taste
2 tablespoons minced parsley

Drain the tomatoes in a colander for at least 1 hour. Heat the butter and toss the tomatoes until heated through. Season with salt and pepper and stir in the parsley.
Yields 3 to 4 cups.

Pizza Dough

1-1/2 packages dry yeast
1-1/2 cups warm water
   2 tablespoons olive oil
   4 cups flour
   pinch of salt

Combine the yeast, water, and oil and let prove. Add the flour and salt and work to a soft but firm dough. Shape into a ball, cover, and let stand until doubled in bulk. Use for pizza, calzone, or turnovers.

Yields 4 large calzone or turnovers.

Basic
11 *Sauces,*
Butters,
& Doughs

Chinese Yeast Dough

1-1/4 teaspoons dry yeast
1/4 cup warm milk
2 tablespoons sugar
1 cup warm milk
3-1/2 cups flour
1 teaspoon baking powder

Combine the yeast, 1/4 cup milk, and sugar and let prove. Stir in remaining milk.

Place flour on a board, make a well in the center, and work in the milk mixture to make a dough. Place in a lightly oiled bowl, turning to coat, and let rise for 20 minutes. Roll into a 9-inch circle, sprinkle with baking powder, and fold in half. Knead well and let rise 10 minutes. Knead again.

Yields 12 to 20 steamed buns.

Flaky Pastry

3-1/2 cups flour
2 teaspoons salt
1/4 teaspoon sugar
9 ounces butter
2-1/2 ounces lard
1 cup ice water

Combine the flour, salt, and sugar. Cut in the butter and lard to make a mixture like coarse meal. Work in the water to make the pastry.

Yields 2 pounds.

Index